Hinman

MW01067987

The Fruit of Her Hands

Look for more books in the Wilson Family Series:

by Nancy Wilson:

Praise Her in the Gates:
The Calling of Christian Motherhood

by Doug Wilson:

Reforming Marriage

Her Hand in Marriage

Fidelity:
What it Means to be a One-Woman Man

Federal Husband

Future Men

Standing on the Promises

THE FRUIT OF HER HANDS

Respect and the Christian Woman

Nancy Wilson

Canon Press

MOSCOW, IDAHO

Nancy Wilson, *The Fruit of Her Hands: Respect and the Christian Woman*

© 1997 by Douglas Wilson,
Published by Canon Press, P.O. Box 8741, Moscow, ID 83843
800-488-2034

03 04 05 06   9 8 7

Cover design by Paige Atwood

Printed in the United States of America.

ISBN: 1-885767-34-X

To Douglas,
the most fruitful person I know.

The Fruit of Her Hands

Foreword 11

A Woman's Orientation to Marriage 13

Walking With God 23

Respect 31

Principles and Methods 57

Contentment 69

Duties of Homemaking 75

Lovemaking 87

Leftovers 99

Foreword

Nancy and I get along very well which, oddly enough, creates some problems. When two people are so compatible, it is very easy to coast on the strength of that natural affection. The problem with this is that it becomes easy to neglect the essential thing in a good marriage, which is reliance on the grace of God. Over the course of our delightful years together, Nancy has been careful to avoid this pitfall, searching the Scriptures for instruction on how to be a godly wife and mother, and she has been just as careful to ask God to empower her to do what He requires.

Probably the best thing I can bring to this book is the testimony that Nancy diligently practices what she exhorts other women to do. She has been writing on marriage and family for a number of years, and in reading her I have never had to wonder at hypocrisy. There has been none.

Simply getting along is not adequate. Nothing serves but love and obedience; a man and woman are called to demonstrate the covenant relationship between Christ and the church. As Christian women consider how they may stand as godly helpers to their husbands in this high calling, I can do nothing better than commend this book to them. The woman who wrote it has lived with a meathead for twenty-one years and has a great deal of practical wisdom.

Douglas Wilson

CHAPTER ONE

A Woman's Orientation to Marriage

For know this, that in the last days perilous times will come: for men will be lovers of themselves, lovers of money, boasters, proud, blasphemers, disobedient to parents, unthankful, unholy, unloving, unforgiving, slanderers, without self-control, brutal, despisers of good, traitors, headstrong, haughty, lovers of pleasure rather than lovers of God, having a form of godliness but denying its power. And from such people turn away! For of this sort are those who creep into households and make captives of gullible women loaded down with sins, led away by various lusts, always learning and never able to come to the knowledge of the truth. (2 Tim. 3:1-6)

Gullible Women

American women today are indeed gullible. They have been captivated by the lies promulgated by the modern world and have succumbed in many ways to the humanistic mindset. Who are the deceivers? They are lovers of themselves, lovers of money, lovers of pleasure. The modern woman has been deceived, like Eve, and led away by her own lusts from her God-given domain and he God-ordained responsibilities. Loaded down with sin—discontent and envy—she is promised freedom and happiness if she will just forsake her domain—the home—and neglect her responsibilities—husband and children.

What are some of the lies she has been told? Fruitfulness is bad; children wreck the budget and the figure. Marriage is a partnership; submission is for imbeciles. Being a homemaker is for airheads who can't make it in the business world. Women are not designed with a unique purpose, but should and can compete with men on any level. The most important thing is to have a healthy self-image and to have your deepest needs met. If they are not being met by your husband, find someone else. The old femininity is outdated. The new femininity dictates that women should look capable, confident, and, at all costs, young and sexy.

How does this sort of thinking creep into our households? The media indoctrinate us daily. The news berates biblical views of wives and motherhood. Popular film and entertainment programs call women to war against men and husbands. They exalt the "modern woman" and neglect or ridicule the mother at home. A friend of mine was taking an English course at a government university and was told on one of the first days of class that no sexist language would be tolerated in student papers. What was the instructor's definition of sexist language? *Mother.* The class was told that they could not use the term *mother* in their writing, but must use the politically correct term *parent*. In other words, they could not write, "The mother baked the cookies," but must write, "The parent baked the cookies." The feminist agenda is rampant in the government schools from kindergarten through graduate school.

One can easily identify the weak-willed woman who has been lead astray by this damnable teaching. She has sacrificed the children and the marriage, her calling and responsibilities, for her own lusts. She has been deceived and is deceiving others. In her frenzied quest for success and approval from the world, she has lost the very thing she tried to gain: a blessed peace and satisfaction. After the career and the wardrobe and the membership in the health spa and the second car and the vacation, there is still a miserable void. All the romance novels on the rack can't fill it. Where to look? Presto! We immediately have a tremendous market for more deception by way of the latest feel-good psycho-babble. Seminars and books and expensive counseling weekends are the next step. Here she can talk about all of her needs and frustrations. Here she can learn how to cope with lack of fulfillment. Here she can learn how to get back on speaking terms with her husband and children. Or maybe she will be encouraged to divorce and find someone who can meet her needs. The modern woman is the epitome of the gullible woman. She is the captive of all kinds of modern deception, always learning, but never coming to a knowledge of the truth. This is the woman of the nineties.

How can the Christian woman dedicated to serving God in her home resist this kind of propaganda? How can the woman who has compromised with the world get back on the right track? The answer is fairly simple, but not necessarily easy. First we must repudiate the world's agenda for women and seek to understand the Word's agenda for women. This is both a protection and a solution. We must determine to be obedient to the Word of God no matter what it says, with no compromises. This is what it means to be a woman of the Word. We must find out what the Bible teaches about marriage, about children, about men and women and their roles, and then we must be obedient with no apologies, no matter what the cost. Is this radical Christianity? No. This is basic Christianity.

A Home With a View

Have you ever stopped to think about how you view your husband, and how that view affects him and affects you?

Now exactly what do I mean by *view*? *View* means perspective. Perhaps the view from your window is of a dreary parking lot, or perhaps it is a lovely view of the hills or a garden. Sometimes people with a lovely view take it for granted—they fail to appreciate it. Instead of admiring the view, they focus on all the weeds to pull and shrubs to prune. Likewise, some with dreary views lift their eyes to the beautiful sky above, and find that they can be thankful for their view afterall.

So what is your perspective when you look at your husband? When you think of him, when you speak to him, when you pray for him, what is your view? Is it a biblical view? Or is it a humanistic view, tainted by the modern world's views on marriage and homemaking and husbandry? And what is the biblical view of husbands anyway?

In the Song of Solomon we see a delightful view of the beloved: "Like an apple tree among the trees of the woods, so is my beloved among the sons" (2:3). When you think of your husband, is he an apple tree in the forest? He should be. Or do you see one tree in the forest, dwarfed by many other imposing trees of greater stature? Perhaps you need to adjust your view.

First you must view your husband as your head. His authority as your head is established in God's Word. "Wives, submit to your own husbands, as to the Lord. For the husband is the head of the wife, as also Christ is head of the church; and He is the Savior of the body. Therefore, just as the church is subject to Christ, so let the wives be to their own husbands in everything" (Eph. 5:22-24).

I would like to emphasize the following two words in the above passage: *own* and *everything*. You are to view your *own* husband as your head. Men are not the heads of women, but husbands are the heads of their own wives. A woman is *not* to submit to other men, but to her own head. A woman must not view other men as her head, but only her own husband. This is important. My husband is my head. I must go to my own head, submit to my own head in all things. I must not run to someone else's head for counsel and help before I first go to my own!

Once when my husband and I were speaking with a couple, the woman asked my husband a question that seemed innocent enough. But I could tell by the man's expression that she had already asked him, and he had already answered her. She must have been unsatisfied with his answer or she would not have been asking for another opinion. What if my husband had given an answer contrary to the one given by her head? That would have put her in a position of wanting to submit to my head and not her own. I pointed out to her that she had dishonored her head by asking my husband what she had already asked her own. Instead, she should have asked her husband if it would be all right to get another opinion on the issue. Then she would not have been setting up a potential problem of pitting her husband against mine and apparently agreeing more with my husband.

A head is given to a woman for protection, safety, and shelter. We must not run from the safety of our own head to what looks like better shelter to us. This is a dangerous temptation and women succumb to it in many different ways. Sometimes they fall by reading Christian books or listening to Christian teachers. "But surely that cannot be wrong," you say. Yes, it is, if they begin to look to someone else *as their head*. Women are readily deceived. What a great protection it is to have a head to submit to, rather than being swayed by our own emotions, whims, and fears. A woman must cultivate a very high view of her head— both the *position* God has given him over her, as well as the *authority* God has given him. When women adopt this high view, submission is seen in an entirely different light. Submitting to someone whom God has placed over you with loving authority is a relief, not a burden.

The second word is *everything*. Hmmmmm. What does *everything* mean exactly? Maybe we can get out of this by examining the word in the Greek. . . .

When we begin to see that God's commands for us result in *our* good, that He has in His divine wisdom provided a perfect plan for marriage, then our fear of submission will diminish. We need to see submission to our own head as a God-ordained means to our protection and happiness.

Of course, some will immediately think of extreme cases where submission would be impossible. I am not talking about submitting to your husband if he tells you to violate God's express commands. I am talking about everyday submission. Submission means the act of yielding or surrendering, deferring or giving way. It is a positive thing, not a negative thing. We are to be obedient to our own husbands as it says in Titus 2:5. This means in all things. Yes, regarding the household, the finances, the children's discipline, education, training, and so forth. What does your head think about these things? How does he want you to handle situations that arise? Does he want you to ask your parents, in-laws, friends, or church elders before you ask him?

We need to cultivate a high view of our husbands and a high view of their God-given jobs. Begin to view your husband as an apple tree in the forest. He is one of a kind, and God has prepared special work for him to do. You have the privilege of being God's appointed helper for him. Have a high view of this calling and a biblical view of your responsibilities associated with this calling. Your view will improve as you apply God's teaching. Your husband will appreciate your obedience and be set free to live up to all God has called him to be. You will find yourself living in a home with a lovely view.

True Ministry

Having a biblical view of headship is a protection in many areas, including some areas in which women may not think they need protection. Consider the role older Christian women have in ministry. Scripture encourages older women to teach younger women to be husband-lovers and children-lovers (Tit. 2:3-4). What does this look like in the twentieth century, given modern media and transportation? Are there any limits to a ministry that a woman may have to other women? What are the dangers and blessings associated with teaching women?

First of all, notice that the nature of the teaching in the Titus passage is very home-centered. This is not narrow; it gives women a very broad spectrum of subject matter that can be covered. Teaching women to be "into husbands" and "into kids" must include many topics, ranging from personal holiness to methods of education. Just about any aspect of the faith taught in Scripture can be useful to the wife and mother. Any Bible-centered study could be used as a real tool, because a good Christian woman will be a good wife and mother.

But what other principles are laid out for Christian women that can come to bear on this subject of women in ministry? Today we have women in the Christian world who write books, edit women's magazines, travel on speaking tours, have radio or television shows, lead seminars, *etc.* If the teaching itself is biblical and Christ-centered, is it automatically to be assumed that the ministry is biblical and Christ-centered?

The first question to ask and answer is, "Who is this woman's husband?" Next we must ask many subsidiary questions. Is she fulfilling her ministry to him? Is he her priority? Is she helping him? Is her house in order? Is he leading her in this ministry? Is her identity as a Christian woman centered, under Christ, around her relationship to her husband? Certainly if a woman is a widow or unmarried, she can have a fruitful ministry. But she will still need protection and accountability of some kind, which should come through the church.

But if the answer to any of the earlier questions is "no," then her ministry is likely independent of her husband, much like a separate career. Yet because it is "Christian," it is somehow seen as a valid ministry. In contrast, because Scripture teaches that the husband is the head of the wife, a Christian woman in ministry should be seen as under her husband's visible headship. In other words, her ministry should be visibly connected to him. This can be a real help to him, for her teaching can be a complement to his work. He can protect her from becoming too committed to ministry outside the home; he can see objectively whether she is keeping her priorities straight; he knows how she is doing spiritually and whether she is even qualified to teach. He can protect her from many temptations and lead her in her ministry to other women. This protection is a blessing. When people listen to or read her teaching, it is organically connected to the head God has placed over her. This is obviously difficult if her husband is always across the country, or if his name is merely listed in the book with the other "credits" in the fine print. This is why I rarely travel to speak at women's conferences, but rather teach where my husband is speaking. Not only does this keep us together, working as a team, but he is then available to continue to lead me and protect me in ministry settings. My teaching role is a support and complement to his, not the other way around. This way my ministry is visibly connected to my husband's and is not seen as a separate work.

Scripture teaches that a wife is specially created by God to be a helper to her husband: "An excellent wife is the crown of her husband" (Prov. 12:4). When a woman in ministry becomes successful independent of her husband, many temptations will accompany such success. She will be tempted to put her "ministry" ahead of her first calling as a wife and mother. She will be tempted to find more satisfaction and gratification in her "ministry" than in her calling to be a wife. Then comes the temptation to accept more and more speaking engagements, to like the financial independence, to work harder outside the home, to get used to being successful apart from her husband, and to become more independent of him.

In some cases, a husband's career is considered inferior, being not as lucrative, so the husband quits his job to manage his wife's "ministry." This is completely backwards. How can we expect God to bless a ministry that is in essence run by wives and supported by husbands? This is especially tragic when the wife's career is Christian in name and is teaching about being a "home-centered" wife.

Women have often been vulnerable to deception, and frequently they are self-deceived. The woman who sacrifices her own home, while teaching other women to be respectful and submissive wives, has been deceived and is deceiving others. This eventually becomes apparent when we read about the divorce. She has torn down her house with her own hands (Prov. 14:1). By the time she recognizes the trap she is in, it is often too late. To quit and go home would be a public scandal; to openly confess sin would be humiliating; to ask for help would be to admit weakness; to fold up the ministry might put other women (or men) associated with the ministry out of a job. She realizes the cost is too great, so she continues to live the lie.

The Church today needs godly teaching for younger women. It must come from godly older women. But godly older women need to be submissive to Scripture and submissive to their husbands first. Then, in a husband-honoring context, they are protected from the hazards and temptations of the "ministry."

CHAPTER TWO

Walking With God

Being a Woman of the Word

> For whatever things were written before were written
> for our learning, that we through the patience and com-
> fort of the Scriptures might have hope. (Rom. 15:4)

At my wedding, my father-in-law, who presided over the
ceremony, prayed that I would be a woman of the Word
and a woman of prayer. After twenty years, I am still chal-
lenged and convicted by these words. Oh, to be a woman
of the Word and a woman of prayer! It sounded so simple
at the time!

As women take on their responsibilities in marriage
and mothering, it is tempting for them to think that a verse
or two a day will do. The demanding schedule may press
Bible reading time to a low priority. There is so much to
do! But keeping in the Book will equip women to fulfill
their ministry to their husbands and children (2 Tim. 4:5).
It will also enable them to discharge their duties before
God joyfully.

Not all women are natural students. It takes discipline
to read the Scriptures. It is easy to put it off until all the
tasks are done. By that time, though, you may be too ex-
hausted to read at all, or your mind may be so filled with
dozens of details that you are unable to pay attention to
even a single word of Scripture that you do read.

We all need help and encouragement to get us into the Book and to help us to become real students in Christ's school. As the Puritan writer Jeremiah Burroughs put it, "Take a scholar who has great learning and understanding in arts and sciences; how did he begin? He began, as we say, his ABC, and then afterwards he came to his Testament and Bible and to his grammar, and afterwards to his other books." We need to begin becoming serious students of Christ, which must begin with simple reading of Scripture.

John Bunyan, in *Christian Behavior,* said, "The whole Bible was given for this very end, that you should both believe this doctrine and live in the comfort and sweetness of it." How can we live in the sweetness and comfort of doctrines if we don't know what they are? We must learn them first, and then we can live in the joy of them. If we are only exposed to a dab of doctrine here and there, this is impossible.

Begin with a very basic plan to get through the New Testament. If you read approximately ten chapters a day, you will read the New Testament once a month. If that is too hefty, read five chapters a day. Sit down and time yourself while you read straight through five chapters (without backtracking or rereading). You will be surprised at what a small amount of time it takes. And that small amount of time would take you through the New Testament once every two months. If you do not understand something, keep going. You'll be rereading it again soon. When I finish, I jot down the date so I can see how often I have been through each book and also tell if I am "avoiding" sections. You can do the same thing by checking off chapters on a Bible reading chart.

You will find that the Lord will bring to mind the Scriptures you are reading while you are working, teaching your children, visiting your friends. Once it has become a pattern in your life, it will bless you very much. The Scriptures are a source of comfort, as Bunyan says, and the doctrines contained are very sweet indeed.

Christian wives tend to leave the "fat books" and theology to their husbands. While this may look "submissive" to some, it is actually disobedience. It is not enough that we know Proverbs 31, Ephesians 5, 1 Peter 3, and 1 Corinthians 1 and 14. We have to know more than how to be a good wife. After all, our first calling is to be good Christians, and if we are good Christians, we will be good wives and mothers, as I mentioned earlier . We musn't be afraid to study topics other than those which directly deal with being a wife and mother. We see in Scripture that women became disciples along with the men. What is a disciple? It is not a mindless follower. A disciple is a *student*—someone enrolled in the class.

This can even be seen in passages of Scripture which some have sinfully misunderstood and written off as "anti-women." When Paul prohibits women from teaching men, he (in the same breath) requires Christian women to be students of the Word. "Let a woman *learn* . . ." (1 Tim. 2:11).

Because biblical learning is required of us, we ought not to be afraid of it. We must overcome our ignorance! Along with Bible reading, we must avoid bad teaching, whether it is on TV, in Christian books, or from the pulpit. We must seek out good teaching. We ought to read good, solid books on Christian doctrine. It is good for us! We must cultivate a taste for books that will build us up in the faith—not take us to fantasy land.

You might want to start with biographies of saints greatly used by God in the past. *Be selective.* Look to your husband for suggestions. Pick up booklets from your church booktable—they aren't too intimidating. Work your way into more and more solid Christian literature. Just read a page or two at a time if need be, and never at the expense of your Bible reading time.

If you miss church, request a tape. Take sermon notes, jot down questions, and afterwards ask your husband questions. (This raises the question of how a woman is to learn when her husband refuses to lead spiritually, but that subject is addressed elsewhere in this book.) Burroughs asks his readers how many sermons they have heard, and how many sermons they have *learned*. The more you read, the more you will find your thoughts and conversation reflecting your reading, and the more you will want to read. Knowing the Scripture will also safeguard you from your mother Eve's vulnerablility to deception. May we all increasingly become women of the Word.

Women and the Serpent

> But I fear, lest somehow, as the serpent deceived Eve by his craftiness, so your minds may be corrupted from the simplicity that is in Christ. (2 Cor. 11: 3)

This verse presents the simplicity of the gospel of Christ in sharp contrast to the craftiness of the serpent. Eve was led astray and deceived by the shrewdness of the serpent. She believed a falsehood and lost the blessed simplicity that is found in Christ.

What is this simplicity? It is not complex, not complicated, not elaborate, nor is it sophisticated. But when it comes to deception and craftiness, the more complicated and intricate the lie, the better. The more sophisticated it appears to be, the more it appeals to the unwary believer.

When the serpent beguiled Eve, he offered her something new and different: "You will be like God." He also contradicted God by saying, "You will not surely die." The serpent flattered Eve into thinking she knew something her husband did not know. Have you ever wondered why the serpent didn't go after Adam instead of Eve? Paul teaches that women are more easily deceived than men (1 Tim. 2:14). The Bible teaches that this is one reason why God has ordained man to be the head of the home.

He is not as likely to be beguiled as the wife. This obviously does not mean that men have no moral problems; men are more capable of outright rebellion (as demonstrated by Adam's disobedience). But women are more capable of being led astray, all the while having good intentions.

Certainly men can be deceived also, but it is more often the case that they do the deceiving, and women do their bidding. One of the most grievous examples of this today is in the counseling industry. When Christian women need spiritual help, they are often too quickly led astray by what passes as "Christian counseling." The counseling explosion is directed at women, and it is sustained by the patronage of women. Women have provided a ready and willing audience for this particular sales pitch. Women have been told all kinds of horrendous lies at seminars and retreats, and even through the latest bestsellers at the local Christian bookstore. What kinds deception are women falling for today?

One popular idea is that your problems are all your parents' fault anyway. You are not responsible for your own faults, because your parents are the ones who brought you up—and they did it wrong. What has happened to the doctrines of forgiveness and holiness? What has happened to that obscure verse somewhere about honoring your father and your mother? (God didn't really say *that* did He?) Like the first woman, we still listen to that particular line, "Did God really say. . . ?"

Or if He did say it, He must have meant something else. He must have had someone else's parents in mind. We flatter ourselves into thinking that God's Word must not apply to our very own special problem, because we are so unique. And this is the same old deception that Eve encountered with the serpent.

Another lie masked as Christian "help" is that you should search back into your past to resurrect old hurts and wrongs. Whatever you remember must be true. This ignores the Bible's teaching about the human heart! We are fully capable of rewriting history and assigning the blame wherever we want. Guard against the popular trend in the modern counseling movement to dig up all the hurt and misuse from the past. For Christians, forgiveness is not the final goal, it is the starting point (Mt. 6:14-15).

Because women are prone to deception, we must have our guard up. Everything we hear must be weighed in light of Scripture. So what does a wise woman do who needs spiritual help? Here are a few suggestions.

Go to your husband first. He is your head and he is responsible before God to shepherd and pastor his home, starting with you. Do not go in order to accuse him of his problems; go to him humbly, seeking help for your problem (Eph. 5:23; 1 Cor. 14:35).

If you have gone to him humbly (without any backhanded criticism), and he still does not want to counsel you, or he does not know how to counsel you, get his permission to seek pastoral and biblical counseling (Eph. 4:11-16). When women call me for spiritual help, I check to see that they have their husband's blessing in seeking my advice. If the husband is an unbeliever or a disobedient Christian, I still insist that she be respectful in discussing the situation.

If he is in outright rebellion himself (*i.e.* a hit man for the Mafia), a wife must not wait to get his permission, but must go get help. As with all human governments, a husband's authority over his wife is genuine, but it is not absolute. There are certain areas of family life where the civil magistrate or the elders of the church have a legitimate jurisdictional interest. So if your situation is a drastic one, you may seek outside help—but still do so respectfully (Acts 4:19).

Do not share your spiritual problem with all your friends. Sometimes talking about it just makes things worse. Many women are simply running their husbands down, and all in the name of seeking counsel and encouragement from friends. If it is not big enough to share with the elders of the church (or the police), so that they may step in to deal with your husband, then it is not big enough to share with anyone. And even if you are unnecessarily silent in a situation, you probably need the practice (Prov. 31: 11). Unfortunately, women frequently share things with people who are not in a position to help, and those who can help(such as the pastor or elders) are the last to find out.

Remember that there is no problem in the world that is new. My husband calls many spiritual problems "off the rack, K-Mart" problems. In other words, they are basic problems with straight-forward biblical solutions. Yours is not unique, and there is always a biblical answer for it. God has not left you without hope. But the hope He offers is found in His Word (Eccl. 1:9; 1 Cor. 10:13).

So be obedient to the Word, and weigh your husband's counsel, or the counsel of your elders, in the light of God's Word (Acts 17:11).

This is not something you can do unless you are very much in the Word yourself. In many situations, it is no wonder we don't know what to do—*we* aren't in the Word. How can we know what God requires if we are not reading what He has written (Deut. 8:3)?

Don't allow the counseling world (even the Christian counseling world) to label your problem with some fancy name. Calling it a *syndrome* does not change anything. Sin is sin is sin. So if the Bible identifies something as sin, then confess it and repent of it (1 Jn. 1:9).

Stay away from books that get you to look inward instead of away from yourself to Christ. He is all-sufficient for all the problems a married (or single or widowed or divorced) woman might have (Heb. 8:1).

Especially stay away from books that get you to think that you have problems that you never knew you had before. Do not be fooled by the line that you are uncovering "denial" (Gen. 3:5).

And finally, pray that your mind will not be led into

deception and corruption, but will stay, remain, and dwell in the simplicity that is found in Christ.

CHAPTER THREE

Respect

Respect Makes a Difference

Let the wife see that she respects her husband.
(Eph. 5:33)

Sometimes I wonder where the Church would be today if the men in it were respected as they ought to be by their wives. What power would God unleash through godly men who were respected in their homes? I am certain that lack of respect and, in some cases, overt disrespect are holding many men back.

Some women are puzzled by this command to respect their husbands. They think respect is simply an emotion, and if they do not "feel" it, then there is nothing they can do about it. Yes, respect is a feeling, but it is also something we choose to do. A dictionary definition of respect demonstrates that it is a verb; it is something that involves action on our part: "To feel or show honor or esteem for; consider or treat with deference or courtesy; to show consideration for." Take note of the words *honor, esteem, deference, courtesy.*

Respect is something that is displayed by the way we treat our husbands. Even if we feel it, we must not stop there but go on to *show* it. And if we do not feel it, we are still commanded to show it.

Oftentimes those wives who disrespect their husbands

are the same ones who are complaining about the lack of leadership they see in their men. If only wives could see the importance of respecting their husbands! Respect equips them, encourages them, and brings great blessing to the entire family: "An excellent wife is the crown of her husband, but she who causes shame is like rottenness in his bones" (Prov. 12:4).

Wives underestimate the impact they have, both for good and ill. They do not realize that their lack of respect is tearing their husbands down. The more they disrespect, the more they see to criticize. Soon it seems there is nothing respectable about their husbands at all.

They want their husbands to be obedient Christians who exercise godly, loving headship, but they refuse to be respectful wives. "I will begin to respect him when he starts exercising spiritual leadership!" But God has commanded wives to respect and honor their husbands, with no qualification. He does not say to respect them *if. . . .* And we know that all of God's commandments result in blessing when they are obeyed.

I have talked with women who were miserable because of the shortcomings they saw in their husbands. I have also seen some of these same women repent of their sin and begin to respect their husbands in concrete ways. Their discontent disappears and they become happy, radiant Christian women again. It is amazing! The blessing that results from simple obedience to God's command is wonderful regardless of change in their husbands.

Wives, instead of focusing on your husband's problems and shortcomings, look at *what you are supposed to be doing yourself.* I have seen the transformation in women as they begin to respect their husbands, and I have no doubt there are great blessings for the husband. It must be a tremendous relief to come home to a sympathetic and encouraging wife, rather than a critical, unhappy, self-centered one. When wives repent of their disobedience and begin to obey God's commands for marriage, blessing always results.

Sometimes a wife must begin to respect her husband out of sheer obedience—even if she does not *feel* like it. But as she obeys God, she also begins to see things she never saw before. She realizes, for example, that he is a hard worker and provides well for the family. It has been wisely stated, "Obedience is the opener of eyes."

Discontent blinds women to the many good qualities in their husbands. When gratitude and respect are cultivated for their husbands, wives find more and more to respect. Conversely, without repentance and obedience, they see less and less to respect.

In *Robinson Crusoe*, Daniel Defoe wrote, "All our discontents about what we want appeared to me to spring from the want of thankfulness for what we have." If only wives would be grateful for their husbands and respect all the good things about their men, they would soon stop moaning and complaining about the things they do not see.

Thankfulness drives away discontent, and respect and honor build the husband up. Even if the husband is an unbeliever, 1 Peter 3:1-2 tells us that he can be won over by the chaste and respectful behavior of his wife. In other words, the Bible teaches that the behavior of wives has a big impact on husbands.

I am not trying to make this too simplistic, saying that if you respect your husband, all your troubles will go away. But frankly, *most* of them will. Begin with repentance before God, ask for His enabling, and begin to admire, honor, and respect your husband. It will soon grow to be a joy.

A Respect Letter

Women are by nature doers. We love practical teaching much more than theoretical teaching; if we cannot apply it, then what good is it anyway? That is why I do not often see women reading big fat theological books, but rather practical books on marriage and child-rearing. (This book is yet another case in point!)

God has obviously gifted women to be "hands-on". We can anticipate needs. We know instinctively what a sick or frightened child needs, what a lonely friend needs, what a busy mother needs. So when it comes to rearing children or homemaking, most of us are thoroughly in our element.

But when it comes to respecting husbands, women need more than just teaching on the fact of the command. We want to know *how*. How are we to obey a command to respect? What are some tangible ways to show respect to our husbands?

In the previous section I defined respect as "showing honor or esteem, treating with deference or courtesy, and showing consideration for". I also pointed out that respect can have happy results in the home. Now I'll offer some do's and don'ts to make it practical. Let's begin with some don'ts. All of these have to do with the tongue. Proverbs 14:1 says, "Every wise woman builds her house, but the foolish pulls it down with her hands." Although I have never actually seen women literally ripping down their homes, I have seen women tearing their homes apart with their tongues. You can almost see the house collapsing as some women talk. It is far too common to hear wives complaining about the shortcomings of their husbands.

Christian wives, never downgrade your husband to anyone—not to friends over coffee, not to your children, not to your parents, and, of course, not to your husband. Do not share your husband's weaknesses, problems, blunders, sins, poor decisions, or failings with anyone. It is disrespect if you do. He is not perfect, we all know that. But when you share unwisely, it does two things: it causes you to disrespect him more, and it causes the hearers to think less of him, too. Sharing his problems is totally unproductive unless you are talking to someone in a position to help (*i.e.*, your pastor).

Never rub in his mistakes. This is a simple application of the golden rule. Do you want him sharing your faults with his friends at work? Of course not. Proverbs 31:11-12 says, "The heart of her husband safely trusts her; so he will have no lack of gain. She does him good and not evil all the days of her life." Can your husband safely trust you? Do you bring him good? A critical, biting tongue is destructive. "An excellent wife is the crown of her husband, but she who causes shame is like rottenness in his bones" (Prov. 12:4). You do not want to be like a disease eating away your husband's strength!

When a husband is openly criticized and disrespected in his own home, he may find ways to spend less and less time there. Some men give themselves more to their work, because at least at the office they are treated with respect. Eventually, some may even get in adulturous relationships because they are bitter toward their wives and looking elsewhere for what they need. This is not a justification of the husband's rebellion, for he is fully responsible to God for his sin. But it does recognize the important role a wife has in her husband's life. She may drive him away with her sharp tongue, and he may find the "corner of the roof" more comfortable than his own home.

What do you do if you have been freely critical of your husband, in speaking to him or to others? First you must admit that your disrespect is sin against God. You have violated His explicit command. Repent of your sin before the Lord. Ask your husband for his forgiveness. You may need to repent also of resentment toward your husband and confess to the Lord that you have been keeping a record of your husband's wrongs. You may also need to tell your friends that you have wronged your husband and betrayed his trust by sharing inappropiate things at Bible study, at the prayer meeting, or in casual conversation. After you have done some spiritual spring cleaning, you will be ready to take concrete steps to respect and build up your husband.

How to begin? You must communicate to him that you respect him, and you need to tell him why. Maybe you should make a list of "rights". What do you appreciate about him? Come on, there must be *something*—after all, *you* married him.

If it is difficult to simply tell your husband you respect him, a respect letter is a very wise way to start. Women know how to write love letters, but a respect letter is another thing entirely. Itemize the things you admire about him, and be sure to include the obvious things you may have taken for granted. Is he a good provider? Is he a hard worker? Does he take the family to church? Has he been faithful to you? Is he kind to his parents? Is he a good father? In most Christian homes, the answer to many such questions is *yes*.

But what about the women who have to answer *no* to all such questions? Then what? If he is at home in front of the TV drinking beer all day and ignoring the family, then you have a harder task ahead of you; but you are still required to respect him. In extreme cases, you must simply respect him for his God-given position as the head of the family, even if he is a poor head. My husband calls this "saluting the uniform". In other words, even if the man wearing the uniform is doing a poor job, he is still worthy of your respect simply because he is your husband.

Apply the golden rule again. Do you want to be loved only when you are lovely? Then do not respect only when you see respectability.

Most women can find many things to respect about their husbands; they merely need to be reminded of the many good qualities that they have been taking for granted. Write him a letter and leave the love out until the end. List to him all the things you appreciate and admire, even if they seem trivial to you. Emphasize his work (or job) first, and then move on to other things. Concentrate on abilities and achievements. Men are very task-oriented; take this into account.

Then begin respecting him verbally. Tell him what a good job he is doing. Thank him for working hard. Thank him for providing for the family. Thank him for coming home to you night after night. Be grateful. Let the kids hear you praise him. Let the neighbors and your relatives hear you praise him.

God has designed your husband to need respect, and He has commanded you to be the principal source of it. As you obey God in this, you will see that an obedient respect for your husband will always have positive consequences.

Still More Respect!

Let's say you have read the last two sections, you have even written a respect letter to your husband, and you are watching what you say about your husband to others. What now? Is there any more to respect than this?

We live in a culture that is becoming more and more disrespectful of, and downright antagonistic to, authority. Children do not respect their parents. How often have you seen episodes of disrespect and disobedience in the grocery store or a restaurant? Students do not respect their teachers and principals. This is blatant among teenagers in America's government schools, but it is also evident among younger children. I have seen little kids holler disrespectfully to adults driving by or to older children walking by. Remember how you used to look up to the older kids?

Certainly the Bible is not respected in our culture; neither the Church nor its pastors are looked upon with regard. Marriage, motherhood, fatherhood, and the family are not honored. Our governmental officials are not respected. Given the shabby state of reverence, honor, and respect in our country, how can women learn to render respect and honor to their husbands, and how can we teach our children to respect authority when there are precious few examples to point to?

The best thing we can do is look to Scripture to see
how godly women of the past respected their husbands.
We can look, for example, at Sarah, Ruth, and Mary, the
wife of Joseph.

Sarah is mentioned in 1 Peter 3:5-6:

> For in this manner, in former times, the holy women who
> trusted in God also adorned themselves [with a gentle
> and quiet spirit], being submissive to their own hus-
> bands, as Sarah obeyed Abraham, calling him lord, whose
> daughters you are if you do good and are not afraid with
> any terror.

It would seem odd to many modern women to call their
husbands "lords," but the fact remains that, if we want to
be Sarah's daughters, we must imitate her respect and
obedience to Abraham.

Ruth is another example of a submissive, respectful
woman who trusted in God. It is clear from the biblical
story that her respect of Boaz was something she brought
into the marriage and not something he coerced from her.
She rendered it to him because she feared the Lord.

Mary is probably my favorite example. Whenever an
angel appeared to Joseph in a dream, off the two of them
went. Not only is this a good example of submission, but
it is also a good example of how God leads a family through
the husband. Each time God wanted to move the family,
Joseph got the message, and Mary trooped long. Think
of what was at stake:

> "Joseph, son of David, do not be afraid to take to you
> Mary your wife, for that which is conceived in her is of
> the Holy Spirit. And she will bring forth a Son, and you
> shall call His name Jesus, for He will save His people
> from their sins. . . ." Then Joseph, being aroused from
> sleep, did as the angel of the Lord commanded him and
> took to him his wife. . . . Now when they had departed,
> behold an angel of the Lord appeared to Joseph in a

dream, saying, "Arise, take the young Child and His
mother, flee to Egypt, and stay there until I bring you
word; for Herod will seek the young Child to destroy
Him." When he arose, he took the young Child and His
mother by night and departed for Egypt, and was there
until the death of Herod....(Mt. 1:20-21,24;
2:13-15a)

This passage teaches us that God moved Joseph, Mary,
and their Son through the obedience of Joseph, and the
submission of Mary to Joseph. She obviously recognized
his God-appointed headship, and she respected it:

But when Herod was dead, behold, an angel of the Lord
appeared in a dream to Joseph in Egypt, saying, "Arise,
take the young Child and His mother, and go to the
land of Israel, for those who sought the young Child's
life are dead." Then he arose, took the young Child and
His mother, and came into the land of Israel.
(Mt. 2:19)

I have been struck by the fact that God did not choose
Mary as an individual to bear His Son, but Mary the be-
trothed wife of Joseph. Joseph must have been a very godly
man, for God chose him to be the earthly father of Jesus
and husband and head of the mother of Christ. God en-
trusted His Son to the care of Joseph. Now Mary could
have questioned Joseph's decisions, but she did not. Imagine
your husband waking you up in the night and telling you
to pack quickly because you are moving to another country! How obedient and submissive would you be? When
they went to Bethlehem, they did so because God had
ordained that His Son would be born in Bethlehem. This
had been prophesied hundreds of years before (Mic. 5:2).
God accomplished His purposes through this godly man
who oversaw the family.

God holds the father responsible for the family. A wife
should, therefore, expect to get wisdom from her husband. God will lead the family through the husband, just

as He lead Mary and her Child through the obedience of Joseph. When a wife understands this biblical principle of family headship, it can be quite freeing.

When I talk to a woman about a problem or a question, I often check to see if she has asked her husband about this first. In many cases she has not. This makes a big difference in how I counsel her. I do not want to advise her in a way that does not recognize his headship. She needs to go to her husband and see if he wants her to talk to me in the first place. Maybe he would rather she did not. God will honor this kind of respect.

Because the husband is responsible for the decisions of the family, a wife must maintain an attitude of respect and submission in communication. You are to honor your husband. He is not one of the kids or your younger brother! Take his responsibility seriously, and he will begin to also. Give him your input, ask for his counsel and advice, and then pray for him. This will free him to be the man God wants him to be, and the man you want him to be.

When women love God and love their husbands biblically, men who have been reluctant to take leadership begin to feel the weight of their responsibility. When the wife is seizing the responsibility, he does not necessarily feel the need to fulfill his obligations. And women don't really want the responsability after all. If you are a daughter of Sarah, neither do you.

Sarah's Daughters

> For in this manner, in former times, the holy women who trusted in God also adorned themselves, being submissive to their own husbands, as Sarah obeyed Abraham, calling him lord, whose daughters you are if you do good and are not afraid with any terror. (1 Pet. 3:5-6)

The context of this wonderful passage is Peter's exhortation to wives to be submissive, chaste, and inwardly beautiful by means of a "gentle and quiet spirit" (1 Pet. 3:4). We can be very grateful that God in His kindness to us had His servants include directions specifically to wives. God understands our frame; He speaks directly to our needs and weaknesses. Here in 1 Peter we have much teaching in a very few verses. Peter links our beauty with the hidden person of the heart, and he tells us that God considers a gentle, quiet spirit to be a precious thing. This is how we are to "adorn" ourselves: we are to trust God (vs. 5), be submissive to our own husbands (vs. 5), do good (vs. 6), and be unafraid (vs. 6). These four imperatives are not only important individually, but they seem to be linked.

The holy women in former times trusted in God. What does it mean to trust God? To trust God is to lean on Him, to rely on Him: "Trust in the Lord with all your heart, and lean not on your own understanding; in all your ways acknowledge Him, and He shall direct your paths" (Prov. 3:5-6). When we trust God, we cease to trust ourselves; we cease to rely upon worldly wisdom. A woman who trusts God is able to acknowledge that all things are under His divine control. A heart that trusts God is a heart that is in submission to God. This trust is based upon God's character. We are able to trust Him because we know that He is the author and finisher of our faith (Heb. 12:2), and because we know that our justification rests solely and completely on the finished work of Jesus Christ. When we trust God, we acknowledge that "all things work together for good to those who love God" (Rom. 8:28).

A woman who trusts God is able to submit to her husband. Why? Because God is in control of all things, even her husband. A woman who trusts God wants to please Him. God has commanded submission: "For this is the love of God, that we keep His commandments. And His commandments are not burdensome" (1 Jn. 5:3). Trust in God frees us to obey Him without regret or worry. Where there is worry, there is no trust. A woman can submit to her husband, even if she thinks he is wrong, because she knows that a sovereign God rules over all to His own purposes. Consider what Joseph said to his brothers when they fell down before him: "But as for you, you meant evil against me; but God meant it for good, in order to bring it about as it is this day, to save many people alive" (Gen. 50:20). A woman does not commit herself to submit to her husband if he makes no mistakes. She submits to her husband because she knows that God does not make mistakes!

Within this context of trust and submission, a woman is capable of doing good. Women may do good in countless ways, and Paul shows us several examples. Bringing up children is the first listed in 1 Timothy 5:10. Obviously, a woman who trusts God and submits to her husband will be far more equipped to bring up her children faithfully than the woman who does not. Personally, I am grateful that God looks on my labor in bringing up my children as a means of "doing good." I am grateful that He sanctifies even the most seemingly mundane tasks! 1 Timothy also mentions lodging strangers and washing the feet of the saints as another means of doing good. This means that all our hospitality can be pleasing to God, whether it is extended to those inside or outside the church. Finally, the apostle mentions relieving the afflicted. This general heading can cover all kinds of service.

Notice the order of these good deeds. Our children are first. Next is hospitality. Then comes relieving the afflicted. The wife does not have to go outside her domain to "do good." The home is the center of her activities, and these activities can be and should be pleasing to God.

Peter commands a woman who trusts God, submits to her husband, and does good, to be unafraid. The three prerequisites are very important. Trust in God is a great protection from fear because we see God in complete control of our lives. The more a woman studies the Word and comes to understand God's character, the easier it becomes to trust Him. Submission frees a woman from many fears if it is rendered in an atmosphere of faith and trust in God. Recognizing that the husband is responsible for his decisions can free a wife from anxiety. Doing one's duties, doing good in and from the home, is another protection from irrational fears. A woman who is busy at home is not an easy prey to shadows and terrors. In our modern society, women are frequently told by the media to be fearful. We are regularly barraged with statistics about women—how many die of breast cancer each year, how many have a rough time through menopause, how many lose their husbands to other women, how many are mugged, how many are killed in car accidents, *etc.* And in case this is not enough, we can worry over our children—how many are kidnapped, get rare diseases, and so forth. This is a set-up for fear and worry and anxiety. Do bad things happen in this world? Of course. But do we believe that God is in control or not?

Phobias are given fancy medical names instead of just being called sin. We cater to fears instead of dealing with them biblically. As Christian women, we need to respond biblically, not emotionally. We can worry about many things that can lead to fear. Fear drives out the gentle, quiet spirit that is so precious in God's sight. We are all vulnerable in different areas, but we are not without a Savior, Christ our Lord. A woman who trusts in God can rest in her submission to her husband and can do good in her calling as a wife and mother. This puts her in a position of strength, enabling her to be like Sarah, who was "not afraid with any terror."

Your Slip is Showing

We've all had it happen or at least seen it happen. Someone gives you that look that says, "Your slip is showing." And off you go to hitch it up.

This seems an appropriate metaphor to use in describing certain kinds of unseemly conduct which, just like your slip, you don't want publicly viewed. There you are with a group of women when you say something that betrays an unsubmissive or disrespectful attitude toward your husband, or you just leak information that really should have remained private between you and your husband. If it's only your good friend or your mother who has noticed, it's not so bad. You can "hitch up" your attitude, confessing your lack of discretion. But what if you are trooping about in full view of the church? The results can be humiliating.

What exactly am I talking about? It can apply to many things, but the general idea is this: sometimes private things that ought not to be shared are shared in full view of the public. Of course this can cover a multitude of topics and can vary from one woman to another. Let's consider a few examples.

Your husband wants you to homeschool your five-year-old. You are not sure you are up to it, and you tell him so. He still wants you to do it and says he will direct the course of study and be responsible for the outcome. So you begin with trepidation and ask your friends for prayer, because, you tell them, he doesn't understand how busy you are already with three preschoolers underfoot and another on the way. He doesn't understand what a hardship it is, you tell your friends, asking for prayer. Your slip is showing.

You have two lovely children. Your husband wants a couple more. You tell your friends that it is easy for him to say because he doesn't have to be pregnant, he doesn't have to take care of them all day. He doesn't fully understand. Your slip is showing.

You have four lovely children. You find out that you are pregnant! You let everyone know, when you tell them your news, that this one was not planned, insinuating that you have more sense than to plan another baby. Your slip is showing!

Your finances are tight; in fact, you are in real financial difficulty. You tell the girls over coffee how difficult it is and how you tried to talk him out of buying that new truck. But would he listen? Your slip is showing.

One thing each of these examples has in common is a complaining spirit. And not coincidentally, the husband is the bad guy in each example. That is the nature of the case. When things are not "water tight" at home, a little discontent, a little grumbling, can leak out.

Once a woman told me her marriage was faltering and asked me if I would be her counselor. I asked if her husband knew she had called me. No, he didn't. I told her to ask for his permission first and call me back. She called back; he had said, "No." I encouraged her to honor him as her head and trust that God would provide someone her husband would approve of to help her. This is a case of a slip adjusted.

Am I saying that women can never share their troubles? Yes and no. A wife should share her troubles with her husband's blessing, in a way that is honoring to both God and her husband. Let's rewind the scenarios described earlier.

Your husband wants you to homeschool your five-year-old. You are not sure you are up to it, and you tell him so. He still wants you to do it, and says he will direct the course of study and be responsible for the outcome. So you begin with trepidation and ask a couple of your friends to pray, telling them how privileged you are to have a husband who will lead you and encourage you. Your husband encourages you to talk to Mary, who has homeschooled for years, for ideas and suggestions.

You have two lovely children. Your husband wants a couple more. You do not say a word about this to your friends until you are up to speed. You tell your husband that you want to be in agreement with him, but you are not yet there emotionally. You ask him to teach you, to please remind you of those things you already know (*i.e.,* the blessing of children), and to help you catch up with him. Then, after you are up to speed, there is really no need to tell anyone. You have four lovely children. You find out you are pregnant. You are surprised! You thank God for His blessing. You surrender your "plans" for the next nine months and get grace to welcome this new precious child. Then when people ask you with one eyebrow cocked, "Was this planned?" (as though it were their business, you can truthfully and gladly respond, "Of course! God plans each child, doesn't He?"

Your finances are tight. You confess your anxiety to your husband and to the Lord. You resolve to trust God and pray for your husband, and you pray for patience. Meanwhile, you show a brave spirit and a joyful countenance to your family, and a creative flair in the kitchen. "I've found a new way to cook beans!" You hunker down and think of creative ways to respect your husband.

Is this to minimize real difficulties? Am I assuming Christian homeschooling moms are supermoms? No. But God is faithful. He honors obedience. He forgives our sin. He never said it would be easy. On the contrary, "count it all joy when you fall into various trials" (Jas. 1:2), and "rejoice in the Lord always" (Phil. 4:4).

If your slip is showing, let your husband point it out in the privacy of your home (or a tactful, loving friend), before you get inside the church door. Don't go out in public with your slip showing.

Respect When It's Hard

> Let the wife see that she respects her husband.
> (Eph. 5:33b)

> Dead flies putrefy the perfumer's ointment, and cause it to give off a foul odor; so does a little folly to one respected for wisdom and honor. (Eccl. 10:1)

Wives are commanded to see to it that they respect their husbands. Husbands were not commanded to see to it that their wives respect them. The command is directed to the wives themselves. Certainly this does not mean that the wife's conduct regarding respect is outside the husband's jurisdiction; but it does appear that Paul's injunction is worded in such a way as to lay the responsibility squarely in the wife's lap. He says, make sure you do this. A wife is to see that this duty is accomplished. Women see that the laundry gets done, that the meals are prepared, that the children are clean, and that countless other tasks get done, but are they as diligent to see that they respect their husbands?

Respect is a demeanor that should characterize wives in all their conduct toward their husbands and in all their communication to or about their husbands—this means courtesy in the home, where the husband is treated with honor. Remnants of this honor from a previous era are our traditions of Dad seated at the head of the table, Dad carving the turkey, [the American custom of] Dad having his own big chair, Dad leading the family in thanks at meals, and Dad doing the driving on the family trips. These are things that we assume culturally, but they come from the time when everyone knew and understood that Dad was the head of the house. Christian wives must show respect by treating their husbands with honor and courtesy in their role as head of the family. They must also show respect in many little ways each day that demonstrate that they revere their husbands in the role God has given them. This can mean following through when your husband requests something, instead of putting it at the end of the to-do list. It can include everything from when dinner is scheduled, to what kind of greeting your husband gets, to making him a cup of coffee. This kind of respect is simply a courtesy which springs from gratitude and love.

Respect in communication includes how wives talk to their husbands and how they talk about them. This kind of respect is also shown on a daily basis. When wife speaks to husband, she should not speak as though she were talking to one of the kids. Her tone should be courteous and kind, not critical, sharp, or flippant. Likewise, when her friends hear her speak of her husband, they should note that on her lips is the law of kindness, not railing and complaining. Rather than sharing his weaknesses, faults, or problems, she should speak of him kindly, saying things that would please him to hear her say. Consider Proverbs 31:12: "She does him good and not evil all the days of her life." This husband receives positive blessings from his wife every day. "The heart of her husband safely trusts her; so he will have no lack of gain" (Prov. 31:11). Again, this husband is confident in the character of his wife; she brings him nothing but good things. He knows she is not telling others things that she should not. His heart is safe with her. She is trustworthy. This is a blessed husband because he has a respectful, courteous, kind wife who lovingly considers his interests ahead of her own. What husband wouldn't be thankful for such a wife? In fact, the husband in Proverbs praises his wife, for she is a source of tremendous blessing for the whole family.

This is indeed a lovely picture. But not all husbands are easy to respect all the time. Difficult circumstances can arise, and the faithful Christian wife may find it a challenge to respect her husband. Consider the quotation from Ecclesiastes above. When an otherwise respectable man behaves in a foolish way, it is a stench. The Scripture does not deny that stupid behavior is unbecoming to a man. It is a foul odor. What does a wife do when her husband is behaving in such a manner, and everyone knows it is folly? Perhaps the stench has traveled far and wide. How can a Christian woman render respect in such circumstances?

Folly can include financial irresponsibility, laziness, unwise comments, irrational behavior, poor decisions, or faithlessness in many areas. The Scripture speaks clearly about sin and does not require wives to pretend their husbands haven't acted foolishly when they really have. Wives must view their husbands' folly the same way Scripture does—as a stench. Nevertheless, respect is still required from wives; it is not a qualified commandment.

A wife may speak to her husband about his behavior. She may ask him to consider what he is doing and encourage him to put things right by making appropriate restitution. She may do this and still be fulfilling her duties of respect and submission, particularly if she speaks kindly and is not bitter and resentful of his behavior. If he persists in his folly, she may need to speak with her pastor or the elders about the situation. This is not disrespectful if it is done with the proper attitude and demeanor. Perhaps church discipline is in order, and the elders are unaware of his behavior. Certainly a wife can do the right thing in the wrong way. For example, it may be her duty to go to her pastor or elders, but she must guard her tongue and communicate about her husband in a respectful manner. Often women think nothing of telling their friends about a situation that they would never dream of telling their pastor. This is backwards. The friend is probably not in a postion to do anything about the problem, while the elders are. It may be disrespecting the husband to tell the friends but may actually be respecting him when the wife goes to the proper authority.

This is not to recommend wives calling their pastors every time a husband slips. If a woman did that she would soon be hearing from her pastor about her own problem. It is merely to point out that God has established a chain of command. If a woman has appealed to her husband about an area of disobedience that he refuses to address, it may be her duty to apply to her pastor or elders. This is not being a tale-bearer if it is done in the proper, respectful manner. It is merely applying respect when it isn't easy. Remember that respect and submission are not what your husband requires of you, but what God requires of you.

Respect and Finances

> He who heeds the word wisely will find good, and who-
> ever trusts in the Lord, happy is he. (Prov. 16:20)

> Every word of God is pure; He is a shield to those who
> put their trust in Him . (Prov. 30:5)

Your trust, your faith, your hope, your confidence must
be in the Lord. You must trust God. Women who follow
the biblical pattern of submission and respect without trusting God are simply baptizing manipulation.

What does such trust look like? You present your husband to God and ask Him to do the changing. You must
recognize that only God can effect a change in your husband. You certainly can be used as His means, His tool to
bring about change, but only if you are in submission to
God and His commands. This should cause great humility
on your part, as you recognize that it is out of your hands.
Your job is to be a humble and willing servant, recognizing that God is at work, and He will bring to pass His will,
using His appointed means. This should encourage you to
pray for your husband, rather than nag him.

Instead of feeling sorry for yourself, thank God that
you have a husband. Thank Him that He is at work to do
as He pleases. Thank Him for the opportunity you have
to apply your Christianity, to live out your beliefs in a
very practical way. You can be stirred up, not only to prayer,
but to humility, obedience, trust, and faith.

Do not look for instant results. Sometimes God brings
about change instantly, while other times it is a slow process. Being submissive to God means you do not have
specific expectations other than the goodness and glory
of God. So expect great things, but do not determine ahead
of time exactly what those great things are. God knows,
so you must be patient.

When you are tempted to criticize your husband (and

you will be), when you want very much to "let him have it," pray for love—"Hatred stirs up strife, but love covers all sins" (Prov. 10:12). Turn to the Lord for comfort, strength, *silence*!

When you believe your husband is acting foolishly or unwisely, go away to another room if necessary and ask God to give you the grace not to "preach" at him. If he asks, gently and respectfully give him your input, looking at your own faults and sins. Are you really better? Had God not intervened, where would you be? This is all the more impetus to prayer.

If he makes a decision you disagree with, you are called to submit. Do so unto God and humbly ask for His protection: "The name of the Lord is a strong tower; the righteous run to it and are safe" (Prov. 18:10).

Now I want to address a specific area in which women have trouble submitting. What if your husband fails to provide for you? What if you are hopelessly in debt, and he is not bringing home an adequate paycheck? There are several temptations you need to avoid in this situation.

First, do not seek to protect him from the consequences of his folly. Even though you may want the Lord to "wake him up," most wives do not want the Lord to be *too* rough on their husbands. We want to shield the blow, ease the hardship, or take on some of the responsibility ourselves. But this will only drag out the problem. You must allow the consequences to fall on his shoulders, no matter how hard it may be for you to watch. I am certainly not suggesting you take a morbid delight in seeing your husband go through difficult times. Of course you must be a support and help and source of encouragement. But that is a completely different thing than trying to shoulder responsibilities that are not yours. When a wife tries to bear the responsibilities that her husband should be bearing, she suffers. (And obviously when abdication includes desertion, a wife must take on many financial responsibilities—she really has no choice.)

So how do you do this? When the bill collector calls, hand your husband the phone. But do so respectfully, praying that God will use it to bring about a change. When there are overdue bills, look to him for his direction—whether or not he provides it. Of course this must be done without guile, without any condemning edge in your voice. Quit scrambling, trying to come up with funds to meet deadlines. It is *his* responsibility.

Have you called your parents and asked for loans? If anyone does this it should be he, not you. Are you trying to find an extra job so that you can keep the house, boat, car? Often women rush into jobs to "help out," thinking it will only be short term. The kids are farmed out because "it's just until we pay off the car." But then, after the car is paid for, there is something else. And pretty soon, you are working outside the home full-time, the kids are on their own, and you are still in debt. Then it is too hard to quit—who will pay the bills? You need to get out, go home, and take care of your kids.

"But," you say, "my husband wants me to work." I have heard this before, when, in fact, the husband wanted very much for the wife to come home, and she was the one resisting the move.

Some of you may find this too hard. You may simply write this off—"She doesn't know *my* situation," you say. But Paul has this word for you: "I have learned in whatever state I am, to be content: I know how to be abased, and I know how to abound. . . . I can do all things through Christ who strengthens me" (Phil. 4:11-13). The context of this passage at the end of Philippians shows that it is a discussion of finances.

So do not think your happiness lies in how your husband is doing, or in how many possessions you have. Your happiness and joy lie in Christ alone. If you are trusting in Him, He will see you safely through.

Without a Word

> Likewise you wives, be submissive to your own husbands,
> that even if some do not obey the word, they, without
> a word, may be won by the conduct of their wives, when
> they observe your chaste conduct accompanied by
> fear.(1 Pet. 3:1-3)

This section is addressed to women who are in the difficult situation of being married to men who do not obey
the Word. I am speaking to women who cannot look to
their husbands for spiritual teaching or counsel, because
they are either unbelievers or they are Christians who are
just dragging their feet. Isn't it wonderful that God in-
cluded in His Word a special exhortation to women in
this particular situation? There have always been some women
who were married to men who "do not obey the Word."
This kind of situation is nothing new.

The first obvious thing about these verses in 1 Peter
is that wives are to be submissive regardless of their husbands' spiritual state. *Be submissive.* While no human authority is absolute, the command as stated here has no
conditions. Notice first that the submission is directed to
your *own* husband. Sometimes women whose husbands
are not obeying the Word can be tempted to be in a submissive relationship with someone else who is more spiritual. This is disobedient and dangerous! Be submissive to
your own husband, and not to your girlfriend's husband
or to your pastor or your counselor. Although we are to
be submissive to our elders in the church (collectively),
that submission is not the same as the submission you render
to your husband as your head. If you are looking to a "head"
other than your own, *you are in a spiritually adulterous
relationship* and you need to repent of it immediately. It
will certainly not help your relationship to your husband
to be looking for headship elsewhere.

Sometimes repentance may be required on another level.

Did you know he was a non-Christian when you married him? Did you know that he could not lead you spiritually when you married him? Did you think you could change him once he was your husband? You may need to do some soul searching here and repent before the Lord for marrying someone He had forbidden you to marry. "Do not be unequally yoked together with unbelievers. For what fellowship has righteousness with lawlessness? And what communion has light with darkness?" (2 Cor. 6:14). Obviously, if you were a non-Christian also, you should remember to thank God that He picks us up where we are, and not where we should have been. (And if you sinned in getting into the marriage, divorce is *not* the way to make it right.)

There are some other hindrances to your submission. One is self-pity. You must stop feeling sorry for yourself and complaining out loud, or just "in your heart", about his lack of spiritual leadership. Grumbling and whining are the enemies of submission. Do not focus on his shortcomings and failings, and stop comparing him to other husbands. This only feeds your discontent and self-pity. Instead, be grateful to God for your husband and begin to focus on his good qualities, even if they are not the ones you want him to have.

Notice in verses one and two of 1 Peter 3 that the thing which wins a disobedient husband is the conduct of his wife. Her conduct is described as chaste and respectful (accompanied by fear). In other words, the thing that will win your husband is your godly and humble behavior. Now think for a minute about your behavior, and ask yourself if you have been acting in a way that will win your husband. Does he see your godliness on a regular basis? I am not asking whether he sees you reading your Bible or Christian books, or going off to church or Bible studies.

This prescription for submissive behavior is not one that applies only to wives who are married to disobedient husbands; it is convicting for women who have godly husbands who exercise a spiritual headship in the home. All wives need a good dose of 1 Peter 3 regularly!

We cannot leave this passage without spending a little time on "without a word." It is difficult for women to do much of anything quietly, much less something that involves changing their husbands. But it is very important that you do not nag your husband. If you have asked him if he will do daily devotions with the family, fine. But do not keep asking. Concentrate on your own behavior, not his. You can read the Bible for yourself, and you can read it to the kids while he is busy with other things. You may joyfully read and study on your own, as long as it is not seen by him as a competition for your time. In other words, do not leave him for the weekend to go off to a women's retreat unless it is something he really wants you to do. You have been designed by God to be his helper, and you can't do this if you are not around.

Flaunting your spirituality is not being quiet. ("I hope he sees that at least I am reading my Bible, even if *he* isn't.") What he needs to see is your sweet and courteous attitude, not how many books you are reading or how many prayer meetings you attend each week. Leave the results to God. This is not a formula to "win your husband to Christ in three easy steps." You are to be obedient to God regardless of the results. The results are His responsibility, not yours.

CHAPTER FOUR

Principles and Methods

Be At Peace

Women who want to be at peace with other women must come to understand the very important difference between principles and methods. A dictionary defines a *principle* as "a basic truth, general law, or doctrine used as a basis of reasoning or a guide to actions or behavior." A Christian woman must learn to think biblically; she must derive her basic principles of living from God's Word. The world eagerly presses its principles regarding marriage and child-rearing upon us. But if we learn to think like Christians, we can discern between worldly and Christian principles.

A *method*, in contrast, is "a procedure or way of doing something." In other words, we use methods to apply our principles. For example, consider this sound mothering principle: all Christian mothers should feed their babies. This principle could easily be substantiated in Scripture, and few, if any, would take issue with such a fundamental principle. In spite of general agreement on this and other related principles, however, much disagreement exists on the method of applying this simple precept. Some women breastfeed their babies; some bottle feed. And of course there is the question of schedule feeding vs. nonschedule feeding, when to wean baby, and so forth.

Within a Christian community, families will certainly share many common principles, but their methods will vary. Sometimes an overzealous allegiance to method will lead to confusion and controversy, for the method of feeding baby can become larger and more important than the principle of feeding baby. Suddenly, pressure is exerted to convince women to join the group and support a particular method.

Of course, this is not an argument that all methods are equal—they are not. Some methods are inferior to others. Rather, the point is that the methods of others are not really our business. If a friend asks for advice on a method, we may of course give it. But when sharing a method, we must remember we are not on a moral crusade.

Young Christian women are particularly vulnerable to this wrong kind of pressure. When the sisters get together, they very naturally "talk shop" about children. This can provide the overzealous type quite an opportunity to apply pressure. If the young women feel inexperienced, a woman with "a strong case" for her method can exert a great influence. The young Christian woman can be made to feel that she isn't really dedicated unless she adopts "the method."

Because every family is a distinct cultural unit, it is good that our methods differ. God did not intend for us to walk in lockstep with one another. This is not altered when some families have inferior methods; we may deem their methods to be unwise. And remember, there are others, wiser than we, who see the inferiority of some of our methods! We ought to rejoice in a common commitment to biblical principles and in the variety of methods God's people employ.

If we become overzealous for conformity to our method, strife between Christians will commonly result. I have talked to women who, because they felt strongly about one way of feeding babies, became critical toward their sisters who used a different method. This should not be! "Be at peace among yourselves" (1 Thes. 5:12-13).

Certainly the women of the church ought not to be squabbling about whether or not to schedule feed their babies! Who cares? What someone else does in this regard is no one else's business. It is not a moral issue, and we have no business fighting over it.

Another example of this crucial distinction between principle and method regards education. Christians must agree with the biblical principle that parents are responsible before God for their children's education. Now if one family chooses to homeschool and another chooses to enroll their children in a Christian school, we ought not get worked up over it. If we get defensive for the sake of our method of education, we have missed the first point of the principle that parents are responsible for their own children; they are not responsible for the children of their friends. We do not honor God if we are critical or defensive. How our friends educate or feed their children is not our concern.

The biggest danger arises when people begin to think their own methods of applying biblical principles are more spiritual. If we fall into this trap, then methods become an issue of first importance for us. The result is a feeling of superiority over others who differ. This obviously leads to self-righteousness, envy, jealousy, defensiveness, and quarrels.

One benefit of Paul's exhortation to older women to instruct the younger women is that older women are not as attached to their methods. They remember their principles, and ,in some cases, have forgotten some of the details of their methods. As we grow in grace, may we all learn to discern the difference between principles and methods, relax, and keep the peace when our friends' methods are not our own.

A Hedge of Courtesy

> Finally, all of you, be of one mind, having compassion for one another; love as brothers, be tenderhearted, be courteous. (1 Pet. 3:8)

Not only do Christian women need to distinguish between principles and methods, but they must cease looking for a simple list of "*how to's*" as the guide for Christian living.

Today, in the evangelical world at large, numerous people seem very eager to give us a list of *do's* and *don't's*. Women are particularly vulnerable to such "lists" because they provide a false sense of security. "I'm okay because I'm obeying the rules!" These rules are often presented to us, couched in appealing phrases like "God's way for . . ." or " the biblical view on. . . ." When we adopt a method, it would be preferable to call it *a* biblical approach rather than *the* biblical approach. These rules supposedly tell us how God wants us to approach courtship, birth-control, child-feeding, and child-rearing; we are given rules about how to wear our hair, how much jewlery and make-up we can wear, what clothes we must wear, what foods we may eat, what we can do on the Lord's Day, what kind of music is permissible, whether we may have a television in our home, how and where we must educate our children, whether our sons or daughters may play sports, and on and on.

We must also remember that what we decide to do in the paragraph above is not "up for grabs." God's laws and principles do apply to our lives in these areas. But our methods of obeying the law do not have the same authority as the law itself.

Another aspect of this whole question of different methods needs to be addressed, and that is the question of common courtesy. How do we treat our friends when we differ with them over methods? Do we criticize them behind their backs? The Bible calls this backbiting. Do we openly criticize them? Do we tell them their method is inferior to our own? This can be arrogant or just plain rude. Do we make officially "polite" but loaded comments which express our displeasure and disapproval of their application of God's principles? Do we try to embarrass them to make ourselves look better? This is not courtesy.

Here are a few examples: "Can you believe how often she has to go feed her baby? My baby was sleeping through the night at six weeks." "Your youngest is almost two? You know three children are better than two!" "Why aren't you homeschooling?" "Why are you homeschooling?" Women who feel free to express themselves about such things may have no idea of the damage they are doing. Common courtesy prohibits one woman breezily criticizing another's methods. It also prohibits nosey questions, such as, "Are you using birth control?" In fact, unless someone is asking for suggestions, there are few circumstances when other women need to volunteer them. In a godly Christian home, the methods should be the result of the husband's teaching and convictions with the wife's support and help. This is all the more reason why women should not rudely give input concerning another Christian woman's application of God's principles. She may be cheerfully submitting to her husband's decisions, only to find her sisters stumbling her into disobedience and discouragement.

Can Christian women ever discuss their methods? Certainly! But the hedge of courtesy and good manners should be firmly in place. If it is not, defensiveness and hurt feelings will be the common result.

But if it comes up, how should we discuss methods? First, we should be, as Peter exhorts us, of one mind. We should have the mind of Christ; we should be of one mind when it comes to principles. We should have compassion on one another. This means cutting slack, bearing with weaknesses in one another, overlooking sin, forgiving one another, and, as Peter says, we should "love as brothers" and be "tenderhearted." A tenderhearted sister is not on a soapbox, preaching her method without care for the condition of her sisters. Courtesy means we listen and ask questions (and not loaded questions). We don't interrupt; we don't get impatient and angry. And, if it is a sensitive issue, courtesy demands that we ask no questions and mind our own business! Courtesy requires that we are, as the Puritans would say, tender of one another's names. We don't spread around anecdotes that would harm the name of our fellow Christians.

Courtesy and love and tenderheartedness must hedge us in. We must protect one another's good names and standing, as we bear with one another in love. It is no challenge to "bear with" people who agree with us on every point. But grace is needed to bear with those who have very different ideas and methods than our own.

Home Run

What if I wrote about the spiritual value of scrubbing your floors twice a day and all the health benefits for your family associated with the practice? And suppose it was all backed up with verses in Leviticus, suggesting that this was God's command for women today? What if I then went on to point out that such hard work, commitment, dedication, and sacrifice would reap for you great satisfaction here and a reward in heaven and followed it up with testimonies from women whose families were changed as a result of the practice? I hope you would think I was out to lunch. But unfortunately, some women would probably either begin to implement my suggestions, or begin to feel guilty every time they looked at the kitchen floor.

Today there is no lack of innocent-looking Christian books with friendly titles making the rounds among Christian women which go far, far beyond my floor scrubbing example. They set down absolute "Christian" rules for everything—infant feeding, potty training, television ownership, homeschooling, or hand-washing—as though they had a verse from the Bible for each petty regulation. I am amazed and saddened at how many Christian women quickly adopt these methods and believe they are doing their Christian duty when they make a chore list and post it on the fridge. Did God actually say in His Word that this is the Christian way?

Why is it so many Christian women want a list of rules or a set of directions for every aspect of their lives? And if they find a set of "holy rules" in a sweet-looking Christian book, they adopt it as though it were Scripture itself, even if it says we shouldn't drink pop or that we should begin potty training our children at birth. What is it in us that wants such detailed rules, and what is it that prompts us to adopt them?

The desire for authoritative rules springs from two sources. First, it comes from a desire to please and not mess up. Many women want to color within the lines, they want to be "good Christians," and they want to please God. But they don't want to figure this out by thinking through biblical principles. They just want someone to hand them a list of rules. There is a false sense of security in adopting a method—"so and so's childrearing method." If it worked for them, it will work for you. When you go to bed at night you can feel good about your Christian life.

The "system" can become a source of security. "I am doing fine with God, because today I cut sugar out of the kids' diet, I'm breastfeeding on a schedule, and I'm having my next baby with a midwife at home." Approached this way, a system is false comfort and it is dangerous. Not only is it self-righteousness and works-righteousness, but if this really is God's way, then everyone else who isn't doing it this way is not pleasing God. In fact, they are in sin. This then leads to a feeling of superiority over those saints who do not adopt the "method."

Works-righteousness, a sense of spiritual security based

upon my lifestyle, undercuts justification by faith. Jesus Christ is the only One who ultimately works. His work is perfect; His work is finished. Our salvation is based totally upon His work, and not upon any work of our own, no matter how righteous we may believe our work to be. My work may make my life more pleasant (or painful), but it will not save me or make me any more secure before God. Christ's work alone is our only true security.

The second reason these "how-to" books, these "authoratative rules" manuals, gain such a hearing is that women can be gullible. When you read a statement that your child will grow up to be self-centered and demanding if you feed them snacks between meals, you need to ask an important question, like, "Says who?" Does Scripture require you to serve only carrots and apples as snacks? Is it more holy than serving cookies and milk? Do you look down on your sisters who have a loaded, accessible cookie jar?

Contemporary Christian women, created by God to be responsive, are vulnerable to temptations to be deceived. We must learn to think like Christians and resist the temptation to believe everything we read or hear. Things are not true because they are bound in a cute little book or broadcast on a Christian radio station. We must stop being muddle-headed and be more closely dependent upon the Scriptures. In the light of Scripture, we must look beyond our methods to principles. When we adopt a scriptural principle, our methods (for methods are inescapable) may or may not look like every other family's in the church.

Every form of works-righteousness is rebellious at the bottom. It does not matter if it is tithing spices or praying on street corners or home educating or home birthing—if you are feeling good about your standing before God because of anything you are doing, you are not looking to Christ or trusting in Him.

Christian women must learn that justification is not found in long dresses, long hair, gardening, vitamins, or

herbal medicine. These are all "things indifferent." But if
you are looking to these things instead of to Christ, seeing your acceptance before God because of these externals, or feeling superior to your Christian sisters who have
different methods, then these "things" are no longer indifferent—they have become wicked.

Sidelong Glances

> The older women likewise, that they be reverent in be-
> havior, not slanderers, not given to much wine, teach-
> ers of good things—that they admonish the younger
> women to love their husbands, to love their children, to
> be discreet, chaste, homemakers, good, obedient to their
> own husbands, that the word of God may not be blas-
> phemed. (Tit. 2:3-5)

It is wonderful how God in His Providence provides work
for all the saints to do. Older women whose children may
be grown and gone can find a profitable and fulfilling ministry in the church by teaching younger women. This is a
healthy and natural (and biblical) calling for older women.
Young women desperately need a picture of godly homemaking in a culture that derides and despises the mother
at home.

I have learned much from the example of older, godly
women in the church. They have taught me how to can
peaches, how to set-up for a Bible study, how to hang
wallpaper, how to serve a wonderful meal, and so on. The
older women can be a rich resource for us in the many
tasks women are called upon to do. In our church alone I
can think of women variously gifted in teaching small children, quilting and sewing, money management, hospitality, teaching, decorating, and cooking. There are as many
expressions of these gifts as there are personalities. Each
church will have a variety of women with a variety of gifts,
and they all have something to offer.

Some of the older women are comfortable teaching in

a formal situation (*i.e.*, Bible studies) while others may prefer to minister one-on-one. I know young women who would love to have the wisdom from an older woman, but they don't know where to go. Older women need to be prodded sometimes to share their wisdom.

But there are two important factors that need to be considered when young women are taught. First of all, what exactly is meant by *older*? The passage in Timothy does not tell us what age a woman must reach before she is *older*, but we must assume that she has already faithfully accomplished all she now sets out to teach. In other words, she must have loved her children in order to teach others how to do so. *Young* women need to know how to love their children, and older women must be, if not finished with the task, at least not still steering the oldest children through the perils of toddlerhood.

What difference does all this make? Young women need to be taught, but not necessarily by other young women. Age brings wisdom and maturity which can only be gained through experience. Young women can be very strong in their opinions about what makes a good homemaker, but they can lack the wisdom and understanding needed to teach with balance. For example, young mothers can be very opinionated about how to feed their babies and can unknowingly (or knowingly) put pressure on newer mothers to feed "on schedule." The same thing can happen with regard to schooling choices or meal-planning or housekeeping. Young women can be very excited about "their method" and then express their views too dogmatically. Young women, especially young mothers, are very vulnerable to this type of peer pressure, and they can come to think that their spirituality depends upon whether or not they are doing their shopping or their house cleaning the same way so-and-so does.

Another danger comes in comparisons. If Mary quilts beautifully, and Susan cooks like a gourmet, and Sarah entertains royally, and JoAnn teaches so well, and Elizabeth sews lovely clothes for her children, and Sally's house is spotless and organized, the young wife and mother can feel overwhelmed by what she thinks are standards set for her. She can begin to feel pressure to perform like all these women, and become frustrated by her inability to be all they are. But all women certainly do not have the same gifts or the same desires. Each woman needs to thank God for her gifts and talents and use them to His glory without comparing herself to anyone else.

Do you like to sew and quilt? By all means then, if you have the time and inclination (and fabric), sew and quilt. Do you like to plan your menu for the week or month? Do so! But what if you prefer another style? It is not sin! What if you are a so-so cook, but you are gifted in instructing your children? You are not less of a godly woman for this.

Remember, the older women are *older*. They probably were not always as they are now. It took them years and years to get where they are. So take your time.

Finally, where do husbands fit into this? Your husband may not realize that you are striving so hard to perform, to meet standards others have imposed upon you (or perhaps you have imposed upon yourself in their name). Talk with him about the input you are receiving from the older (or younger) women. Get his perspective on it. Husbands may not care when you shop or whether you take up knitting, so they may be totally unaware of the pressure you are feeling.

Once I told my husband that I needed to get more organized. I was obviously feeling that I was not being that Proverbs woman in some way or another. His response was very funny (and liberating): "What makes you think I'd want to be married to you if you were more organized?" This was very freeing to me! God wants me to be myself in obedience to *Him*, not to someone else. Then I am free to enjoy the gifts He has given me, and to learn and grow from the godly examples around me—"But let each one examine his own work, and then he will have rejoicing in himself alone, and not in another" (Gal. 6:4).

CHAPTER FIVE

Contentment

Self-Evaluation at 11 PM

"If we would have peace in our souls, we must maintain
a war against our favorite sin and never leave off until
it is subdued." —Thomas Watson

While sin in others is often blatant and obvious to us, our
own sins are sometimes disguised. Because we don't see
them for what they really are, we can trick ourselves into
fighting and confessing the wrong sins altogether.

One such sin is morbid introspection. While confessing our shortcomings and sins over and over, and finding
no joy, we fail to see that we are responding to self-accusations, and not to the Holy Spirit. Though we may think
we are being pious (thinking we are such miserable creatures), we are actually indulging in a self-centered, me-focused, self-pitying activity that is not looking to Christ
for grace, strength, and forgiveness.

Consider the following scenario: It's been a long day.
You were up at 5:30 a.m. with the baby, and got a good
breakfast on the table for your husband and kids. Then
you packed the lunches, got the kids off to school, cleaned
up, showered, dressed, fed the baby again, read to the
toddler(s), stopped for lunch, put the little ones down
for naps, baked cookies, folded clothes, watered the petunias, took the kids to the park, listened to the events of

the school day over cookies and milk, fixed dinner, greeted your husband, served dinner, cleaned up, got the six-year-old working on his letters and the eight-year-old working on math, gave four baths, read bedtime stories, snuggled with the little ones, fixed your husband some coffee, and collapsed in a chair to enjoy it with him. After an hour of visiting or reading you can't keep your eyes open. You look at the pile of ironing that didn't get done, and you remember the letter you meant to write but sigh and go to bed.

Suddenly you are wide awake. Now with a quiet moment to think, thoughts flood into your mind. You remember that on top of the unfinished ironing you were short with your daughter when she asked for the third time when dinner would be ready. You confess it to God, but you still feel bad.

You wish you had spent more time coloring with your six-year-old. You remember his look of disappointment when you told him you had to hang out the laundry. Now your stomach is in a knot. What a terrible mother you are, you tell yourself. You don't even act like a Christian. You didn't even read your Bible today, and you haven't for three days. Besides, you've gained five pounds and you look terrible—no self-discipline at all. And if you were really disciplined, you would work out. Your husband is probably unhappy about those five pounds, you tell yourself. And so it goes on.

Hold it! This is not the time for self-evaluation! After a long, draining day, you are not qualified to do any evaluating! This type of thinking, any time, but especially after 10:30 p.m., is unfruitful. It only breeds self-pity, condemnation, hopelessness, and ungodly sorrow. This is an unwise and dangerous mindset to indulge. One sin always leads to a host of others. Introspection leads to anxiety and depression. It is an unfruitful and misleading mindset, for the real sin is not the five pounds, *etc.*; it is the act of engaging in this self-condemning activity. "Set your minds on things above." The real sin being committed is this mindset, this morbid introspection. This is what you are least likely to repent of, for your failures of the day distract you away from the real sin. And this is what needs to be confessed. A godly sorrow produces repentance; a worldly sorrow produces death (2 Cor. 7:10). If you really have sinned (as with losing your temper), then do, by all means, confess it to God. If you still feel guilty and sick at heart, then you may need to get up and make restitution to your child (if she's still awake), or write a note of apology. But then do not dwell on it!

If it is not an objective sin, but an accusation that is grounded on nothing more than vague feelings about the day, dismiss it. God is not the author of accusation and condemnation of His children. He chastises and forgives. He delights to show mercy. He is the Father of all comfort. He does not pile on accusations in the night!

In reality, you will see things much more clearly in the morning. If you think you are a rotten mom at 11 p.m., decide to sleep on it and ask the same question in the morning. You may be emotionally and physically drained and therefore vulnerable to this sort of temptation. In the morning you may feel like you aren't such a horrible mom after all. Remember, it is God's Word that is the standard, not your feelings—good or bad, late or early. In the light of day it is easier to see your weaknesses, call for grace, confess your sins, and thank God for His love and forgiveness. Like other sins, this sin of introspection can become a habit. As Thomas Watson said, "If then, you would show yourself godly, give a certificate of divorce to every sin." When confronted with your sins and failings, look to Christ and thank Him for a perfect justification.

Health Care

> Who exchanged the truth of God for the lie, and wor-
> shiped and served the creature rather than the Creator,
> who is blessed forever. Amen (Rom. 1:25)

If you are an American woman, you live in a culture that not only idolizes health and youth and beauty, but actively promotes the fear of disease and disability and old age. "The ultimate goal for modern man is to be achieved through health and fitness, for only the healthy and fit have fun!"

Whenever the worship of the creature replaces the worship of the Creator God, many truths about the nature of man and the nature of God are necessarily suppressed and replaced with false ones. Lies are the prerequisite for idolatry. This is why the Christian woman must be prepared and alert to ward off the subtle, and not-so-subtle, attempts to deceive her. What are these lies? They may take many forms.

When man ceases to live for the glory of God and lives to glorify himself, death and disease are the great and obvious enemies. The problem for modern, pleasure-seeking, God-hating man is, "How can I worship my body and its pleasures for the longest period of time without the intrusion of sickness, disease, or that ultimate party-killer, death?" As J.C. Ryle points out in his booklet *Sickness* (Gospel Mission Press, 1990), neither the atheist nor the deist has a satisfactory answer for the problem of disease. Only the Christian has a true answer: the world is fallen through sin; the wages of sin is death.

The Christian woman must resist the world's attempt to hold her hostage through fear. Women seem to be the target of much of the media's fear tactics—all in the name of "empowering" women. Perhaps this is because modern women are prime targets for the media. Whether it is through magazine articles, news programs on television, ads and commercials, or the ever-present video in the doctor's office, we are constantly encouraged to fear. Sometimes this fear is used to get us to buy something. A beautiful, gray-haired woman is shown slipping and crashing to the ground. Osteoporosis. They want us to dash out and buy calcium pills. Other times it may be a philosophical argument that we are asked to buy. "You are in charge of your own body," we are told. "You are a new, modern woman who is self-sufficient and independent. You make your own decisions regarding your body. You have a right to know the facts." (I am not making this up. I saw a video like this in a doctor's office just a week ago.)

Now, what is wrong with this? It is humanistic, obviously. It removes God from the picture. Imagine, instead, a video like this: "You are a creature. Your Creator God has made your body, and it is a marvelous creation. Your body is not your own; it is a gift from God. It is fallen and therefore susceptible to sickness and disease. Be a good steward of this gift, and serve God with your body." Wouldn't this be a shocker, given our humanistic mindset? Try to imagine it as a pharmaceutical commercial on television!

Once a Christian woman succumbs to the fear of cancer and heart disease and menopause, the fear, like cancer, spreads. She fears for herself, and because she is compassionate, she begins to fear for her family members. Perhaps statistics are high for multiple sclerosis in your part of the country. Oh no. What can you do? Your state has a high incidence of childhood cancer. Should you move? Your great aunt died of cancer. This puts you in the high-risk category. Your cousin had a brain tumor. Does it run in the family, or was it just a fluke? This is the stuff fear is made of. If I watch my diet and do aerobics, I won't die of a heart attack. Very good. What will I die of then?

Obviously, nothing can keep all sickness and disease away for good. We are all going to die—each and every one of us. And we are all going to die of something. But for the Christian, there should be nothing to fear in this.

"Who shall separate us from the love of Christ? . . . neither death nor life...." (Rom. 8:35, 38). When Christian women get sucked into the fear trap, they are forgetting this important truth, as well as some other important ones. Review your theology to deal with these fears. Sound theology is the cure for fear. Consider that God is in complete control of His entire creation. Do you believe this? Remember that sickness is one of the means God can use to teach His children patience, endurance, compassion, trust, gratitude, and contentment. It can be a refining tool in God's hand. If you are God's child, you can know that He will work all things together for good, and this includes sickness, disease, and death.

Even though you may be the one in the family who makes the appointments with the pediatrician, remember that you are not capable of ensuring the perfect health of your family. You are just a creature too. God may need to remind you of your own finitude.

Of course, the Christian woman can honor God by seeing that the children get their shots and medical checkups and learn about hygiene. God can use these things to protect your family. So much is simply godly prudence and Christian stewardship. But do not rest in these externals; rest in Christ.

Accept the fact that God does allow sickness for His own good purpose. Do not be afraid. Keep away from stories or documentaries that are set-ups for fear. Always evaluate what you are being told. Is it true? Is it being presented in a way that is biblically accurate? Does it take the Creator/creature relationship into account? Because the world worships the creature, this distinction is seldom made. Do not be afraid, but fear God.

CHAPTER SIX

Duties of Homemaking

Joyful Duties

Many years ago I was the busy mother of three children, ages four, two, and under one. Life was full, with hardly time to sit down. I was occupied with many mundane things like diapers and laundry and crayons and play dough. Once in a while I would wonder just what happened to my "ministry" that I had enjoyed when I was single and working with a Christian organization. This was simply the very old "the grass is always greener" temptation.

One night as I was washing the dishes (which was the last hurdle before tucking in the little ones), my mind wandered off in that direction. Shouldn't I be leading Bible studies? Shouldn't I be involved in more active evangelism? Couldn't I "disciple" someone? Didn't God want me to do something for Him?

Immediately I realized what He wanted me to do. He wanted me to do the *dishes*. But I still wondered if there was something *else* He wanted me to do. And I realized that, yes, there was something else. He wanted me to do them *cheerfully*.

As I reflected on this, I realized what I had known all along. God had called me to be a wife, mother, and homemaker. Because of this, all the mundane things I did were sanctified, holy, purposeful, and honoring to God, and I should offer them all to Him. "I beseech you therefore, brethren, by the mercies of God, that you present your bodies a living sacrifice, holy, acceptable to God, which is your reasonable service" (Rom. 12:1). Not only that, I should also find contentment and satisfaction in knowing I was doing these things unto the Lord.

When Christian homemakers view their work in this way it makes all the difference. Work, hard work, no matter how humble the task, is our service to God. If this is true of digging ditches or washing dishes, certainly it is so when it comes to rearing our children. I had a congregation of three right in my home—a Bible school with three students enrolled! When we view managing our home as drudgery, it becomes just that—drudgery. But if we view it as our duty to God, it becomes a joy and delight. I remember my mother telling me that she never begrudged being busy at home because she saw it as her *duty*. If your home is disorganized and untidy, or downright dirty, you are not honoring God in your duties as a wife and mother. We are to learn to manage our households (1 Tim. 5:14). It is our duty before the Lord, and we must do it well.

One time when my children were still very young, a woman stopped by for a visit. "How do you keep your house so clean?" she asked. I thought for a moment, and I remember answering, "I work really hard—*all the time*." What a mystery! What a secret! Being committed to a clean home and clean children rules out many other activities. It can mean little time for novel-reading, not too many long phone calls, and not much socializing. The home and the children are the first priority. Bathing the children, keeping their clothes clean, feeding them, and teaching them are all part of a full-time job that requires planning, stamina, and a heart that is committed to work.

Hard work is good for us. It strengthens us and builds character. Idleness is an evil that is not only destructive, but it is always accompanied by many other sins. It tears down our families and is dishonoring to God. When you are working hard at home, you don't have time to watch degrading television shows, you don't have time to spend your money recklessly, and you don't have time to fritter on the phone. Your hands are too full with your duties—

> For we hear that there are some who walk among you in a disorderly manner, not working at all, but are busybodies. Now those who are such we command and exhort through our Lord Jesus Christ that they work in quietness and eat their own bread. But as for you, brethren, do not grow weary in doing good. (2 Thes. 3:11-13)

Hard work always bears fruit over time. Children who are loved and fed and washed, and who are taught to love God, grow up to become productive saints in the household of God.

Certainly I do not mean by this that work excludes all recreational reading and visiting. Anything can be taken too far. The children are more important than your particular cleaning schedule, and we all need rest. Mothers must be able to know when to lay the work aside. But just as our work is "unto the Lord," so our rest should also be unto Him. This principle helps to establish guidelines for both work and rest. He must bless my rest in order for me really to enjoy it. He must bless my work for it to be truly fruitful.

> And whatever you do, do it heartily, as to the Lord and not to men, knowing that from the Lord you will receive the reward of the inheritance; for you serve the Lord Christ. (Col. 3:23-24)

The Sin of Having to Know

> And besides they learn to be idle, wandering about from house to house, and not only idle but also gossips and busybodies, saying things which they ought not. (1 Tim. 5:13)

This passage refers to the temptation younger widows encounter when they have no husband at home to provide the ballast they need to be home-centered. But certainly, other women in the Christian community are tempted to be busy-bodies as well. It may sound harmless, but Scripture ranks this sin with some of the big ones: "But let none of you suffer as a murderer, a thief, an evildoer or as a busybody in other people's matters" (1 Pet. 4:15).

What is a busybody? In this passage, she is a woman who delights in other people's business. Instead of being focused on her own home, her own duties, her own family, the busybody is interested in everyone else's business. A busybody is "busy" gathering and passing on information. Of course, saying these things is sinful, but knowing them may be equally sinful.

Let's back up and examine how a woman becomes a busybody. First she must *learn* idleness, as our text says. But how does a woman *learn* idleness? The image seems contradictory! I suggest that it is learned by studiously avoiding the duties God has laid out for her. The budding busybody must shirk her domestic duties for the more pleasant task of "visiting."

The woman Paul describes is wandering about the neighborhood. It is far easier to leave unfinished duties behind than step over them. The women the busybody visits can't see her laundry pile or the dirty kitchen floor. As the busybody wanders from house to house, she is far from idle: she is busy gathering information about everyone else's affairs. Does the modern busybody wander from house to house? You bet. She goes here for coffee and there for lunch. She's charging around town, dropping in and checking up. Or she may be busy chatting over the back fence while hanging out the laundry. The news gathered at stop one is repeated with relish at stop two. This also provides her with lots of prayer requests for Bible study or prayer meeting.

Of course the modern busybody is not restrained if she doesn't have the means to wander about town. She has a more convenient method—the telephone. The modern busybody can be very "busy" on the phone for hours a day. This sort of idleness may produce weariness, but it doesn't produce the fruit God requires. A woman's God-given duties must necessarily be neglected to carry on such extensive visiting.

How does the busybody conduct her visits? She asks many questions and is a keen listener. She asks questions that are meddlesome and interfering. But she seldom gives offense because she seems so genuinely interested. No detail is insignificant for her. She delights in passing on "tasty morsels" and offers much information (about others) without waiting to be asked.

Since her head is so full of "other people's matters," much of what is fact and what is hearsay is easily blurred. Now she has become not only a busybody passing on the "news," but a gossip passing on rumors. Meanwhile, is the laundry done? Is dinner planned? Can she really afford all this time?

A few cautions come immediately to mind. First, ask yourself if you are a busybody. If you are working hard at home, faithfully doing your God-given duties, then you will have little time for such foolish behavior. Nevertheless, recall your recent conversations. Have you been too involved in "other people's matters"? Do you ask questions that are really not your business? Do you pass on information about other people's affairs? And perhaps the most revealing question: Do you delight in being the *first to know* and the *first to tell*?

Second, do you have a friend who is a busybody? Take care. You may be drawn into her bad habits. Don't listen to her repeat all the news. Excuse yourself from inappropriate conversations. Do you have a regular group you meet with to "visit" and fellowship with: a homeschool group, a sewing group, a quilting group, or a reading group? Is the conversation on topic, or is it often about other people? Perhaps you should withdraw from such a group, if it is dominated by busybodies. Busybodies will be quick to criticize the children, the schooling methods, *etc.*, of people not in the room. They will share things freely about others that they would never say if those people were present.

Finally, if you know someone to be a busybody, keep your distance. Be careful what you tell her. Assume that everything you say will get around the community. That should motivate you to exercise discretion. Be careful what you say about your family, especially about your husband. Be sure your comments are always respectful and kind and God-honoring. That sort of news isn't nearly as much fun to pass on.

Friends

> The righteous should choose his friends carefully.
> (Prov. 12:26)

Think for a moment about this text. The righteous must not only choose his friends, but do so with care. This requires wisdom. Frequently, Christian women "fall into" friendships on the basis of proximity and compatibility. Someone moves in next door, you "hit it off," and the next thing you know, you are fast friends.

But Proverbs says friendships should be the result of careful choice, not indiscriminate happenstance. Just because you have much in common (your husbands work at the same office, you attend the same church, you read the same books), or just because you see one another often (sitting in the bleachers at the kids' soccer games), does not mean you are wise in establishing a friendship. These may be "carnal" reasons for friendship, not spiritual reasons. "The righteous should choose his friends carefully." This implies using your head to think about the nature of the friendship and the qualities suitable in a friend.

Often women seek friendships that gratify the flesh but do not promote spirituality. For example, maybe you appreciate your friend because she will let you talk without restraint (Prov. 10:19). Perhaps you enjoy someone because her children are just as undisciplined as yours, so you feel no pressure to tighten things up. Does she help you waste time, keeping you from your duties, but giving you a plausible excuse (1 Tim. 5:13)? Does she delight you with morsels of gossip (Prov. 18:8) that you might not get elsewhere? Maybe she has a husband who isn't meeting her needs either, so the two of you can complain about your husbands together. Is she popular, or wealthy, or very gifted, and you just enjoy associating with her because you like to drop her name to others and impress them with your friendship? All of this is abominable. These are examples of unwise, ill-chosen friendships. They either need to be overhauled or ended, but in either case repentance is in order.

There are other dangers associated with friendship. "Do not be overly righteous, nor be overly wise: why should you destroy yourself?" (Eccl. 7:16). This is the problem of the woman looking for a "super spiritual" friendship. This can be a cover for a very lonely and needy woman. She may be reading Christian books, studying the Bible, very involved in Bible studies, or even leading them. But she is not a woman deeply satisfied with Christ; she is looking for a deep, spiritual relationship with another woman and expecting her needs that are unmet by her husband, or not found in Christ, to be met in a "relationship." She wants to share, she wants to pray, she wants to develop a deep, meaningful relationship in a deep and meaningful way. Beware! When it is counterfeit, this sort of spirituality is every bit as dangerous as the gossipy relationships described earlier. Godly Christian women should enjoy friendships that are not replacements for their husbands. If you have a husband, he can and should be your "best friend." If he is not, no woman can fill the void he has left, so don't look for such a friend.

So what is the alternative to these failures in friendship? One important fact to remember is that a woman cannot be close friends with everyone. Jesus had His twelve (Jn. 15:15). From those, He had His special three, Peter, James, and John (Mt. 9:28). And from those three, He had the one whom He loved, John (cf. Jn. 21:20). Christ enjoyed a closer relationship with some, not with all. Surely we may imitate Him in this. Being finite, we cannot have an intimate friendship with an infinite number of people. Besides, we all have many God-given duties, and were we to pursue friendship above all else, our duties would necessarily be neglected.

Within a Christian community, a woman may enjoy many godly friendships on different levels. There may be friendships the older women have with the younger women; these are characterized by teaching and encouragement. In some relationships you are consciously giving (*i.e.,* teaching and encouraging—see Tit. 2:4), and in others you are deliberately receiving or being taught. Such friendships are biblical. They may develop into close friendships, or they may not. Other friendships are possible with "peers"; these are characterized by companionship and mutual edification. All these friends must be chosen carefully.

But how? Obviously, the choice cannot be one-sided, for if the person you select is not interested in a friendship, there is really nothing you can do. Do not be discouraged, and do not resent the other person. She is required to be just as careful as you are. Do not attribute motives! If you have initiated many times, and she does not respond, do not assume that you know why.

Do not set yourself up for a big disappointment either. Trust God to lead you in your friendships. If one does not work out, He must have other plans. Do not ask someone to be your friend. Instead, look for opportunities to develop naturally. Do not force it. Again, God will direct the friendship if it is meant to be. The kind of woman you want for a friend should be a gracious Christian woman. Obviously, you must be the same kind of woman yourself.

A godly friendship ought to bear righteous fruit—it should be productive, refreshing, delightful. If it is not, it is a waste of time. There are many sweet Christian women whose friendship would be rich and precious. Seek such women out. As Proverbs instructs, choose your friends carefully. Do not underestimate the effect of your friendships on your Christian life.

Home Ownership

God has been so kind to us in giving us homes and families to fill them. The earth is the Lord's as is everything in it. Obviously, our homes are the Lord's as is everything in them. It follows that our homes should reflect His ownership in all aspects. Our attitude toward our homes should be one in which we seek to glorify Him in our daily use of the things He has graciously "loaned" to us. Knowing it is His and that He has bestowed it on us should keep us humble (knowing we don't deserve it), content (knowing we don't deserve it), and thankful (knowing we don't deserve it). This protects us from temptations to arrogance, envy, and ingratitude.

Remembering that our homes belong to God should also have a significant impact on the way we manage them and, therefore, on the way they look. A Christian woman ought to be able to apply her Christian worldview, including her view of the family, in the way she cares for, manages, cleans, and decorates her home. After all, if it is God's home, it matters how it looks. We serve a God who is holy, righteous, orderly, not chaotic, and is the Creator of all that is lovely. Surely our homes should reflect this. If He created light, texture, design, and all in harmony, shouldn't our homes celebrate and appreciate His masterly control over all things?

One of the things the Puritans did well was recognize the goodness of the creation. This enabled them to keep God first in their lives while enjoying immensely, with gratitude, all the physical blessings He bestowed on them.

"The Puritans determined to make earthly things divine, not by forbidding them, but by infusing them with holiness" (*Worldly Saints*, p. 208). They could enjoy wealth by realizing it was a gift from God, by keeping it in subordination to Him, and by using it to do good. Richard Sibbes said, "Worldly things are good in themselves and given to sweeten our passage to Heaven" (p. 59).

As we recognize the goodness of God's gifts to us and keep alert to the temptations attendant to such blessings, we are free to use our worldly possessions in a God-glorifying manner. Non-Christians have no concept of worshipping and glorifying God in how they decorate a home. Their only options are self-glorification or guilt in ownership. Only the believer can enjoy material things fully in such a thankful, and not guilty, way.

As the Christian woman takes stock of her resources and abilities, she can be motivated to make her home lovely in a Christ-honoring way. She can seek to make her home beautiful to please God. The pagans may want to impress one another, but the Christian can delight in Christ.

This may provide an entirely new motivation for Christian women to keep their homes clean and organized and to be always working to make them more beautiful, given the resources God has given to them.

Decorating a home should reflect God's ownership of our homes and our lives. Christian women should seek to honor God in the way they pick out furniture and hang curtains. A Christian home should be and look different. This does not mean different because Bible verses are hanging on the walls, but different because it reflects a desire to please God in all of life.

Because women typically are more involved in the actual decorating process, it is important they are careful to acknowledge the presence of their head in the home. A Christian home should be decorated in such a way that it looks like a man lives there, and that his wife is a complement to him, not a competitor. This does not mean a set of antlers in every room, but a Christian wife has the duty to find out what her husband likes. Does he like dark colors? Light colors? Any colors? He may never have thought of it before. He may need time. They both may need to begin thinking about this together for the first time.

Because of the feminization of our culture on many levels, home decorating has sunk, in many cases, to simply lining the walls with hearts and bunnies and tying a bow on everything in sight. This country or Victorian "cute" excludes almost entirely the masculine presence. Certainly a Christian home should reflect the presence of both the masculine and the feminine.

Am I trying to lay down one particular style as "Christian"? Absolutely not. God has created us with tremendous variety, and our homes should reflect this. Not only do we have a variety of tastes, but a variety of circumstances, resources, and differing levels of maturity in taste. But we should all begin or continue in the process, for our homes should be practical extensions of what we believe to be true about God and His world and demonstrate that it is all under His ownership.

Lovemaking

Gardening

If there is one area where Christian women may have a lot of worldly notions and baggage, it is the whole area of sex. This, like many other areas of our thinking, must be overhauled if we want our marriages to honor and glorify God. The first important concept for women to understand is that sex was God's idea, not Adam's or Eve's. It is obviously a gift from God and should be enjoyed within the parameters He has established in His Word. It is a created thing and should not be served as though it were more than that. Like all created things, it can be misused and misunderstood, even by Christians. Because sex was God's idea, He has provided guidelines in His Word for us. He governs the world, including sex. He understands our nature and governs us justly and wisely. When He commands us to behave in a certain way, we must take it very seriously, and not weigh it next to the world's wisdom to see which is more appealing to us. As in any gift from God, there are duties and responsibilities associated with it. So we will examine what the Bible says these responsibilites and duties are.

Paul states one of the purposes of marriage in 1 Corinthians 7:1-5: it is a protection from sexual immorality. God knows our frame, and He has established the marriage covenant as the fence around the sexual relationship. If there is no fence, there should be no relationship.

This is so important for Christians to understand. It is very straightforward and does not need interpretation. Nevertheless, today Christians justify immoral behavior by using many carnal arguments. Engaged couples tell themselves, "Well, we will be married very soon, so God will excuse it." Wrong. This kind of behavior and thinking is destructive in both the long- and the short-term. This is the old ploy from the Garden of Eden: "Did God really say. . . ?" When we begin to mess with God's Word to excuse sin, we set ourselves up for all kinds of evil behavior. The short-term consequences of immorality are guilt, loss of joy, lack of self-control in other areas, and muddled thinking. The long-term consequences are a lack of respect of wife for husband (*If only he had controlled himself*), regret and shame, as well as a wife's concern over her husband's faithfulness in the future (*If he compromised before we were married, will he compromise after, too?*). Engaged couples need to think long-term about their testimony to their children and grandchildren. When their own children someday come to them for wisdom about courtship and engagement, will the parents have to admit their own failure and lack of self-control, but insist that the children "be good"? Engaged couples can be so caught up in the present that they forget that they will ever have grown children themselves. It is far better to hurry up the wedding than engage in immorality (1 Cor. 7:9). Marriage is God's prescribed context for sex; we sin grievously when we fool ourselves into thinking otherwise.

Within the protective fence that a marriage covenant provides, a Christian woman can be free to enjoy the gift of the sexual relationship and learn to enjoy it in a way that is pleasing and obedient to God. For many Christian women this is a difficult task, for they have lots and lots of baggage from the world regarding sex and have picked up plenty of goofy ideas that they must unload before they can have a healthy, biblical view of sex. Of course we should get our ideas from Scripture and not from the latest issue of *Good Housekeeping*. The Song of Solomon is a good place to start. Here the bride is referred to as "a garden enclosed"(4:12; 5:1). Much beautiful imagery in the book refers to this fertile, lush garden with its pleasant fruits. Cultivating such a view is a healthy beginning to developing a biblical view of sex. The garden is a private place for only the husband and wife. It has a high wall around it called the marriage covenant. In fact, in many ways, the husband is the garden tender, and the wife becomes a source of great joy and delight to the husband as he spends time in the garden he faithfully tends. (The whole subject of an untended garden will be dealt with later.) This beautiful picture stands in stark contrast to the world's seductive and promiscuous view where all the gardens are unwalled and men trample through them freely and quite casually. (Women mistakenly think that they are free when they sleep around, but in fact they are being vandalized and misused and left unprotected.)

As a Christian woman begins to see herself as a garden, she can take a more eager interest in making it a lovely garden that her husband delights to spend time in. Think of some of the loveliest gardens you have visited. What was it about them that delighted you? The peaceful atmosphere, the soothing effect on your soul? You want your husband to feel that way when he visits you. A woman who cultivates this view will not be so quick to resent her husband's sexual advances as intrusive. She can welcome him to his garden knowing that he will find it to be a delight, a comfort, and a joy.

How can a woman tend her own garden? By being affectionate, approachable, warm, and responsive. Women know too well how to be cold and unresponsive when they want to be. This is like hanging a sign out on the garden wall that reads in large letters, "No trespassing." But of course a husband is never trespassing in his own garden, though he can be made to feel as though he is an intruder.

A woman with a gentle and quiet spirit is far more approachable and appealing than a woman who is anxious or worried. Being distracted with cares and concerns is not lovely. Keep your garden free from bitterness and resentment. These are foul weeds which choke out your loveliness. An atmosphere of cheerfulness and openness and humility will allow your husband to feel welcome in his own lovely garden.

Satisfaction

> Let your fountain be blessed, and rejoice with the wife of your youth. As a loving deer and a graceful doe, let her breasts satisfy you at all times; and always be enraptured with her love. (Prov. 5:18-19)

This section of Proverbs is directed to husbands, but certainly it has something important to say to wives as well. Did you know that God has commanded your husband to be satisfied with your breasts all the time, and to be enraptured with your love? Are you helping your husband to obey this command?

Notice that the first part of the verse tells the husband to *rejoice* with his wife. Given the context of the passage, it is obvious that this is speaking about rejoicing sexually. He is to keep himself pure by not dispersing his fountain in the streets nor embracing the immoral seductress. Instead, he is to be enraptured by his own wife who is a loving and graceful doe. The sexual relationship between a believing husband and wife should be characterized by *rejoicing*! Isn't that a freeing thought? Christian wives need not be shy or embarrassed or feel guilty about what God has called them to rejoice in. Neither should a wife view sex as a mere duty or obligation, inconvient and time-consuming. No, it should clearly be *joyous*. As I mentioned in the previous section, the wife is a lovely garden, and time in the garden should be a delight.

Can you describe your behavior in bed with your husband as *rejoicing*? If not, you need to think about why it isn't. Adjusting your perspective can often have the biggest impact on your behavior. Next time you approach the marriage bed, prepare your heart to rejoice.

The next important principle from this passage is the command to husbands to "let her breasts satisfy you at all times." Christian men are constantly having to avert their eyes from other women's breasts, whether it is on the covers of the magazines at the grocery check out, in films (which they maybe shouldn't be watching), and, of course, the women who dress indecently at the office or on the street. All those women's breasts are forbidden to them, and it is a regular nuisance to have them constantly thrust in their faces. Only the wife's breasts are not forbidden. These are the breasts they are not only allowed but commanded to enjoy. The question is, how are they to let their wives' breasts satisfy them *at all times* if they can never get near them? The obvious word to the wives is to see that your husbands do enjoy your breasts. This is very clearly connected to your responsiveness and warmth. Is your husband sure of a warm response when he approaches you sexually? Or does he have to prepare himself for a brush off? You are his wife. Your breasts are his to enjoy. Let him! Enjoy his enjoyment of them and do not withhold from him what God has commanded him to be satisfied with. Certainly it is difficult to be satisfied by (or pleased with) something that you have no access to. If you prepared a lovely meal for your husband and set it on the table but would not let him sit down to enjoy it, he would not be satisfied. Even less could he enjoy it if you never got it out of the oven!

The final point to consider is what it means to *enrapture* your husband with your love. This means that you must be more than simply responsive. You must be active in the sexual relationship. You certainly must delight him in a passive sense, but there is more required to *enrapture* him. My dictionary says that *enrapture* means "to fill with intense delight." This implies a great rejoicing on the part of both partners. What you do to your husband doesn't simply delight him; it *fills* him with *intense* delight! The picture is not one of a husband merely getting a green light, but quite a warm reception. He is *filled* with delight. This is not a teaspoonful once a week. It is a picture of a cup overflowing. Notice also that the husband is commanded to be *always* enraptured, not occasionally enraptured. The picture I get is of a husband who is so completely sexually satisfied by his wife that he is (as a friend of mine put it) like a wet noodle. He is not strung up tight sexually because of a feeble sexual relationship, but is married to a woman who makes it her objective to delight and enrapture him all the time.

This may seem like an overwhelming command. It probably is difficult for most husbands to obey it faithfully. The husband's obedience is not the wife's problem. But her own obedience is what I am addressing here. Now I am not telling you *how* to do this. I am simply telling you that you must. It is your duty before God to help your husband in his obedience of this command. You are given to him by God to satisfy him, to delight him intensely, and to rejoice with him. There is an important reason why I am not telling you *how*. That's because you need to ask your husband. He is the only one who can tell you what will delight and enrapture him. Undoubedly, when women take on this task seriously, they find much joy and delight themselves.

Overcoming Hindrances

Developing a biblical perspective toward sex is a great place to start. But even if you believe all the Scriptures say about it, no doubt there will still be obstacles to overcome. Knowing the right thing to do is the first step, but it won't always be easy. The world is always resistant to the truth, and our flesh gets in the way of our good intentions. Let's consider some of the common obstacles that keep a woman from being the responsive, joyous wife who enraptures her husband.

Fatigue is a common excuse for mediocre sex. When a wife has two toddlers and one on the way, by the end of the day, bed looks like it is for one thing only: sleep. This is a genuine problem. Women who take their responsibilites seriously work hard all day long. Taking care of children is not only physically and mentally demanding, but emotionally draining as well. By the time the children are all in bed and the dishes are done, there's not much left to give husband. A wife can see her husband's advances as one more person who wants something from her, and her perspective can get very warped. This calls for a real perspective adjustment. Though taking care of the children is an important part of her calling, it is not the only part. A wife is to be a companion and friend as well as a lover to her husband. She cannot sacrifice all she has to the children and say to her husband, "Sorry, what was yours I gave away to your kids." Fatigue is an obstacle, but not an insurmountable one. Recognize it for what it is. Talk to your husband (or doctor) about possible solutions. Get practical help. Do you need a nap in the afternoon? Do you need to get the kids to bed earlier? Pray that God will give you that second wind in the evening so you can nurture your relationship to your husband. Surely, together you can overcome this one. But do not let it go on. It may be years before you have the energy you used to have before you began having children. Being tired is not a sin! Adjust to your new circumstances and make the necessary changes.

Another common problem is when the wife is "not in the mood." Often during pregnancy and nursing, women simply lose their normal sexual desires. This is not to panic over. Our bodies are fearfully and wonderfully made. Who can understand them? Certainly we cannot understand ourselves very well. Nevertheless, your husband's desire has probably not suffered a dip. This is an obstacle, but again, it is not insurmountable. Sometimes you will have to work harder to "feel like it." It is not always necessary to consult your feelings anyway. I have sometimes compared sex to a meal. Every night cannot be steak and lobster. Some nights it's just macaroni and cheese. But a good cook can make that macaroni and cheese a real treat! If a wife is not feeling "in the mood," she simply has to apply the golden rule. Does your husband always "feel" in the mood for a heart-to-heart chat? Perhaps not. Do you want him to tell you when he is not in the mood but just talking because he loves you and knows you need it? Of course not. A Christian can do his duty simply because it is his duty, and God will bless it. Think of the sacrifices he makes for you, and determine to be a delight and joy to him in spite of your feelings. They are not the most important thing.

Perhaps you have had bad sexual experiences in your past that are a hindrance to you enjoying a healthy relationship with your husband. This can be another hindrance that you must overcome. Remember you are a Christian. Christians are people who understand what it is to be forgiven. We are not to drag our past around like a ball and chain. We have been delivered from our past sins. Thank God for His forgiveness, and do not dwell on your sins. Dwell instead on His grace and mercy. But if you have suffered at the hands of others sexually, you must extend forgiveness. Nothing can interrupt a happy relationship like bitterness, even if the bitterness is toward someone other than your husband. Forgive those people in your past who wronged you sexually and do not allow their sin to ruin your life. That makes no sense at all. Some would have you dig it up and pore over all the wrongs you have suffered. This is unproductive and unhealthy. How many times did Jesus say we should forgive those who sin against us? Countless times. Put your theology into practice and ask God to help you forgive those who sinned against you. This is the necessary starting point in overcoming these things. Don't make your husband suffer for wrongs others committed.

Prudishness is another problem that Christian women may have to deal with. This can be camouflaged as spirituality. The Bible is not a prudish, Victorian book. It is pretty earthy in spots. We must be careful we do not attempt to be holier than God (which of course is a silly idea). If God did not forbid it, why do we? Do we think we know something He doesn't? We are to be *pure*, but not *prudish*. My dictionary defines *prude* as "a person of extreme or exaggerated propriety concerning behavior . . . one who is easily shocked by sexual matters." God has declared the marriage bed to be honorable. So should we. Do not try to conceal your other excuses by pretending to be spiritual. God has made it clear in His Word what types of sexual activity are forbidden. Beyond this, it is a private matter between you and your husband, and it is no one else's business. Often Christian women need to loosen up a little and be willing to talk to their husbands about sex. How else will you discover how to please and delight one another? Do not approach sex as though it is an unspiritual activity. If God has been pleased to call the marriage bed honorable, we should be able to give a hearty Amen! Rejoicing in one another is impossible if you have a feeling that what you are doing is really wrong.

More obstacles will no doubt rear their heads in your married life. But if you are used to acting out of principle and are determined to be obedient to God, these too can be overcome with God's grace and strength. Nothing that is too easy is ever worth much. But if you ask God to help you think and act like a Christian in this important area, He will teach you and lead you in the sexual area. Don't expect sudden, drastic changes. Our sanctification is a gradual process. But you should see progress as you apply His Word.

Untended Gardens

Sadly, some Christian women are married to men who have very confused attitudes about marriage and sex. It is no wonder, though, considering the kind of world we live in today—a world that is mesmerized by, confused about, misuses, and worships sex. Any time a created thing is elevated by man beyond its creaturely status, it becomes severely twisted and deformed and loses its God-intended worth, benefits, and purpose. When Christian women are married to men who are involved, for example, in pornography and view sex as simply a pleasure-gadget, it will be difficult to apply biblical standards to the sexual relationship. Difficult, but not impossible.

Actually, more than one kind of untended garden exists. The wife married to the man described above has a garden that is not seen or appreciated for what it is. That husband tramples the garden and picks as many flowers as he can as often as he can. Soon, of course, the garden is depleted and he wonders what the wife's problem is. Why can't you produce more flowers?

Another kind of garden neglect is the husband that spends little time in the garden. He doesn't plant, and he doesn't care about the weeds, and he certainly doesn't water. He just shows up now and then, looks for a pleasant experience, and then goes his way again. Both of these kinds of gardeners are a grief to their wives.

Now this is not written to men; it is written to women. If you have a husband like the ones described above, you must *not* make the mistake of trying to undertake to deal with *his* sins; you must deal with your own. If, however, he is a Christian man who is engaged in viewing pornograhpy, you may need to go to the elders in your church so he can be disciplined. But if he is simply not spending enough time with you (from your perspective), or is not meeting your needs in some other way, you must realize that God is the only One who can bring about change.

The Scripture is clear that you may be a potent instrument in God's hand, if you are committed to being the woman described in 1 Peter 3 who wins him without a word.

If your husband is an unbeliever, going to the elders may be a help to you spiritually, but they cannot discipline someone outside the church.

Some women need to recognize the fact that they must tend their own garden. Ultimately, our Lord is really the Master Gardener. Husbands are to love their wives in such a way as to make them lovely. But when they don't, wives do not have to throw up their hands in despair and give up! Rather, if you are married to an unbeliever or a disobedient believer, you must determine before God that you are going to attempt as best you can to fulfill all your obligations as a wife in a godly fashion. This means you must apply all the Word's teaching on sex whether your husband does or not. Esther won over the king and was greatly used as a result. Your godliness is never dependent on someone else. You stand before God in Christ and are accountable to Him for your behavior. Perhaps God can use the sexual relationship as one of the means of winning him back to obedience or winning him to Christ.

How does a woman tend her own garden? First, confess all your resentment and bitterness toward your husband. Forgive him for his conduct and his oversights. Ask God to give you the grace to respect and love him when you do not feel like it. Confess your lack of respect for him. Determine to begin treating him with honor, courtesy, and deference. Quit complaining to him and about him. Then you will be in a position to begin to be affectionate and warm and create a joyous atmosphere in the home that will welcome him.

If in doing this your husband only seems to get worse, do not give up. Sometimes things do get worse before they get better. However, if he wants you to participate with him in viewing pornography, you must be clear in your refusal. Your submission to him is always to be in submission to God. What God forbids for His children cannot be overridden by a disobedient husband. Your husband's authority is subject to God's. While refusing to participate with him in immorality, continue to be respectful and not self-righteous. If he continues to wrong you in ignoring you, remember, as an old Puritan put it, it is better to be wronged than to do wrong. Do not wrong your husband in return, but treat him as God would have you treat him, knowing that God sees your obedience and will bless you for it.

Let God tend your garden, and do not let envy for other loved wives or resentment toward your husband ruin yours. And even if your husband does not see it or appreciate it the way he should, if he ever does wake up and open his eyes, he will see a lovely *tended* garden waiting for him.

CHAPTER EIGHT

Leftovers

The Virtue of "Carelessness"

If I were fruitless, it mattered not who commended me,
but if I were fruitful, I cared not who condemned.
—John Bunyan

Criticism. Condemnation. These are not words we like to hear. All of us would rather be praised and appreciated than criticized. But if we are living fruitful lives before God, it is most likely that we will be criticized and condemned by the ungodly world. Conflict with the non-Christian world is a given. How can a godly wife not only bear up under this, but also continue to be a help to her husband and an example to her children amidst such opposition? We should adopt Bunyan's attitude, which is certainly a biblical one. I have by no means mastered this, but I hope I can encourage you with what I have learned by being married to a man who is often surrounded by controversy. The quote I cited above has been and continues to be an inspiration to me.

First we must remember our Lord's teaching that the servant is not greater than the master. If Christ was mistreated, misquoted, misunderstood, and maligned, then we will be—"Do not marvel, my brethren, if the world hates you" (1 Jn. 3:13). We often act surprised when the world maligns us. This demonstrates how far we are from the biblical mindset: "Woe to you when all men think well of you" (Lk. 6:26). We must become more acquainted with our Bibles and with Church history; then we won't marvel when our families are criticized or condemned for the faith.

Of course, we must not by our ungodly behavior give the enemies of the gospel opportunities to blaspheme (Rom. 2:24). If our marriages are not in order, if our children are disobedient, or our homes a wreck, then we give the gospel of Jesus Christ a black eye. Criticism from the outside should be the result of our godly behavior, not our sinfulness. We must be wise as serpents and harmless as doves (Mt. 10:16). What a disgrace to read of Christians divorcing, children rejecting the faith of their parents, pastors forsaking their calling. Christian wives and mothers need to awaken to the need for personal holiness and obedience. Let us receive criticism for our faithfulness and fruitfulness and count it all joy; but if we receive it for our unfaithfulness and fruitlessness, then we deserve everything we get and probably more.

Criticism from non-Christians can come in different forms and degrees. It can range from being funny to being serious. If it is just harmless and funny, we should be able to laugh and not take it seriously. An example of this kind occurred some years ago when my husband wrote a weekly political column for our local newspaper. Someone wrote in with the opinion that my husband was a "total idiot." Initially, I did not think it was very funny. But when my husband chuckled over it and suggested that I write in to say that the critic didn't know the half of it, I started to laugh too. We must consider the source. Then we can say as Bunyan does, "Who cares?"

Another time I heard from friends of an older woman who was criticizing me quite freely to them. She told them how I had thrown my life away by not marrying someone rich. She also told them how I had runny-nosed kids and how I looked like I had been drug through a knothole.

No, I didn't enjoy hearing about this. But what difference does it really make? People like this woman need our compassion and prayers.

But other criticism can be far more serious and result in the loss of a job or promotion. This is not hypothetical; we have seen it happen to friends. We have seen at least one person nearly unable to secure a graduate degree because of his Christian ethics. Another friend was squeezed out of his job completely and had to change careers. This type of criticism cannot be laughed at, but there is a Christian response to it.

The first thing we must not do is react emotionally. That will simply complicate and muddle the situation. We ought first to apply the Scripture that tells us to bless those who persecute us; bless and do not curse (Rom. 12:14). When you pray that God will bless the one who is mistreating you, it is a protection from bitterness. Thomas Watson, in *All Things for Good*, says, "Whoever brings an affliction to us, it is God that sends it." Do you believe this? If you bless and do not curse, you can trust God to work it out for your good and His glory. If you disobediently curse, moan, complain, and wallow in self-pity, you will not see God's blessing.

In blessing, we must also forgive: "Love covers a multitude of sins" (1 Pet. 4:8). We see Stephen's example of forgiving those who were stoning him. And we have the example of our Lord forgiving His executioners from the Cross. This is the Christian standard—"But I say to you who hear: Love your enemies, do good to those who hate you, bless those who curse you, and pray for those who spitefully use you" (Lk. 6:27-29).

This leaves no room for bitterness, resentment, or lingering hurt feelings. You are commanded to do good to those who hate you. This is impossible if you go out of your way to avoid them, and it involves more than just adding them to your prayer list. It doesn't matter if the ones who hate you are family members or only business acquaintances or even strangers. If you do not know them, you can still pray for them. If you do know them, you can look for positive good to do for them, and you can ask God to give you ideas and opportunities. This is Christian love that the world does not understand.

When you come to obey the Scriptures in this, you will be able to agree with Bunyan and truly not care who condemns.

For Widows

> For your Maker is your husband, the Lord of Hosts is His Name.(Is. 54:5)

When young women make their wedding vows, they are seldom pondering how they will prepare for widowhood. And yet, many women, sooner or later, do become widows. My neighborhood is filled with large, older homes that house lonely little widows.

Our Lord obviously had a tenderness for widows; we see His concern for them in His condemnation of hypocrites: "Woe to you, scribes and Pharisees, hypocrites! For you devour widows' houses, and for a pretense make long prayers. Therefore you will receive greater condemnation" (Mt. 23:14). And James reminds us how important widows are to God: "Pure and undefiled religion before God and the Father is this: to visit orphans and widows in their trouble, and to keep oneself unspotted from the world" (Jas. 1:27).

Women need to understand some important principles that will help them now, equip them for later, or just enable them to encourage widows they know. What are some of these principles?

First of all, it is fundamental that every Christian woman comprehend that "your Maker is your husband, the Lord of Hosts is His name." If you are a child of God, you are part of the Bride of Christ. Your Maker is your Husband. Christ is the Head of the Church, collectively, and He is consequently the Head or Husband of each of His elect. If you are a single woman, you have a Husband; if you are a widow, you have a Husband; and if you are married, you have an earthly husband, one who is a picture of your heavenly Husband, Christ. Though Christian wives are commanded to respect and submit to their earthly husbands, they must do so in submission and obedience to their heavenly Husband, Christ. He is your Physician, your Advocate, your Priest, your Shepherd, your Husband. Though earthly husbands may be called away from families through death, your heavenly Husband has promised never to leave you or forsake you. Wives, while your earthly husband is alive, cultivate biblical thinking about this. Good doctrine will be a tremendous help to you in trial. Believing and learning the right things about God are like storing up provisions for a famine. When affliction comes you will have a good store of grace available.

Not only must you have a solid grounding in your doctrine on God's relation to you, you must also believe the right things, the biblical teaching on His control over all things. The Scripture's teaching on His absolute sovereignty will be a comfort and a protection for you if your husband is taken from you. Did God do this? Is He a loving Father? Could He have kept your husband from dying? Why didn't He? It is far better to learn the answers to these questions now. Then when difficulties come, you will not be shaken in the fundamentals of the faith. Store up His promises now, and you will remember them later—like Christian did in Doubting Castle, when he found the key of promise in his pocket. I have a precious friend who is a young widow, and she has taught me much about God's faithfulness to those who trust in Him. His promises are very real to her; they are like a lifeline that keeps her afloat day after day.

After settling the importance of a solid theological foundation for widows, other principles for living must also be learned. One principle is found in Titus 2:11-12:

> For the grace of God that brings salvation has appeared to all men, teaching us that, denying ungodliness and worldly lusts, we should live soberly, righteously, and godly in the present age.

Here we see that we must learn to say "no" to ungodliness. Widows must learn to say "no" in all kinds of situations, and they must teach their children this as well. A husband is a tangible protection to the wife. When he is taken away, she becomes suddenly vulnerable. People who were hindered from being a nuisance by the husband's presence now feel free to say and do what they like. A godly woman must not be reluctant to say "no" to many things. Some may want to devour her household—they must be prevented. A widow cannot be timid about saying, emphatically, *no*. Those believers around her must be an encouragement to her in this area, because saying "no" can at first seem like a rudeness to her. It may seem "unchristian," when in fact, it is the righteous, obedient thing to do.

Widows can find tremendous solace in seeing themselves married to Christ eternally, together with all God's elect. Though the married state on earth can be a blessed one, it is only a shadow of the heavenly marriage of Christ and the Church. In that eternal marriage, there are no widows.

Granny

My mother recently gave me a letter written in faded pencil on yellowed notebook paper. I had sent it to my granny in 1963, thanking her for the pajamas, hankies, socks, and perfume she had sent for my eleventh birthday. The last six lines of page two are filled with x's and o's, affectionate tokens of hugs and kisses. Granny saved my letters, and when she passed on, my mother saved the letters. The penmanship is fair, the content predictable, and the form is self-consciously by the book. Not much worth saving really. But the fact of the letter speaks volumes about something far more important than the weather at girl scout camp.

My parents taught me to love and respect my grandma. That meant writing thank-you letters when I received a gift, as well as writing newsy letters from time to time. I remember my mother (Granny's only child) writing her mom once a week. I also remember the trips to see Granny and her trips to visit us.

Over the years she gradually became cranky. Still my parents would travel a couple thousand miles each year to see her. In between times they called and wrote and sent gifts. The last time they went to visit she wouldn't let my mother even use her washing machine, so my folks went to the laundromat. Shortly after this visit ended, Granny had a stroke. My parents hurried back to take care of her. Mom took her meals (she wouldn't eat the hospital food). After the stroke Granny was more uncooperative than ever. Mom learned to give her insulin shots. Dad sold her house, got a moving van, loaded up all her belongings, drove back to Idaho, and started making preparations for his mother-in-law to move in. Mom stayed until Granny was well enough to travel, and then they flew home.

Mom and Dad were living in a mobile home while they were building their house. Dad rearranged the floor plans so Granny could have a room near theirs.

It wasn't easy. But God never promised obedience would be easy. He did promise blessings and grace and strength, and that is what He gave. My parents had been free to travel, but suddenly they had a fulltime responsibility at home again. Initially Granny was not always pleasant, but God began to work a wonderful change in her. Though her speech remained garbled and confused as a result of her stroke, her heart cleared. She could say a few intelligible sentences: "Isn't that lovely?" "He [meaning my dad] is the sweetest thing!" "This is wonderful." She became a sweetness and a joy. She loved to sing and pray or fold clothes. She was always pleased with meals, and enjoyed watching my dad work outside. Flowers were a delight to her. Mom kept her dressed nicely, her hair always done, her room bright and cheery.

Even so, it was sometimes hard for my parents. They sacrificed some of their best years when they could have been traveling and "enjoying life." Instead they were enjoying Granny, taking her for rides to see the Christmas lights or the flowers in bloom.

When they talked to Granny about her salvation, she always responded in agreement, though her sentences were mixed up. God obviously had intervened and worked a marvelous change in her life. She was not the same woman.

One morning Mom was with Granny in her sunny room. Granny was in her bed when suddenly she looked up and smiled, and reached out her hand. Then she was gone. At first my mother assumed Granny had been reaching out to her, looking up at her. But then she realized that Granny had probably been responding to another presence in the room—she had looked up with a smile and reached out. What a glorious departure!

My parents' love and commitment has taught my family a tremendous amount about what obedience looks like. God was honored through their honor of my Granny. My children received a blessing through their obedience as well, for they not only got to know their great-grandmother, but they saw God transform a bitter old woman (who would have died lonely and desolate in a nursing home) into a sweet little dear. They have seen what a Christian family does for aging parents, and they have seen the "inconvenience" and hardship coupled with the fruit of obedience.

I will always be grateful to my parents for keeping my

letters to Granny, for teaching me to love and honor her, and for honoring and loving her themselves. May we all be blessed to have such children as my Granny had.

Decorated Doorways

Although our culture holds the state of faithful marriage as a thing despised, it still nods in approval at the wedding festivities. Flowers and champagne and fluffy flower-girl dresses, toasts and limos and honeymoon suites are all very much in style. Thoughts of a bride still conjure up beautiful images of sweet innocence and that much-coveted state of being in love.

The world's wedding industry has much to say about what kind of wedding to have and how much a typical wedding should cost, but very little of substance to say about what a wedding really is. This is why Christian moms and brides need to learn to think of weddings from a truly Christian perspective. (Of course it is obvious that Christian dads and grooms must think Christianly about weddings, but this column isn't for them.) After all, Christians more than all people should understand what a wedding is all about. We understand covenantal headship and the blessing of marriage and children. Surely we should have the best sort of weddings, weddings far different from those of the unbelievers. That means Christian weddings should be real celebrations, not boring, meaningless rituals presided over by disinterested officials and attended by duty-bound friends who would rather be fishing.

Christians must learn and rejoice in the biblical significance of a wedding. Otherwise, our children might as well just elope and skip all the hoopla and save Mom and Dad a lot of time, money, and trouble. If we don't understand, then what's the use of all the planning and expense for a twenty to thirty-minute ceremony? Instead of taking signals from the modern wedding industry, Christians need to examine each aspect of the wedding from a biblical standpoint. We need to ask ourselves some very pointed questions about why we are doing this. For just one example, why is Dad walking his daughter down the aisle? In most American weddings, this aspect is assumed but not understood. Christians know that Dad is giving his daughter away. This is in many ways the most significant part of the wedding ceremony. Who gives this woman to this man? The father has assumed responsibility for his daughter as she has grown up in his household, and now he is giving her to her new head, her husband, who will assume this responsiblity for her protection. Christians should not follow cultural traditions blindly, but many of these wedding traditions have biblical foundations.

Before getting into the actual wedding planning, a biblical perspective on the ceremony is absolutely necessary. One of the first things that should be obvious is that the wedding is the entrance into the marriage. The wedding ceremony is not an end in itself. In fact, marriage is not an end in itself. Marriage is a means of serving and glorifying God. Young women who view marriage as their chief goal are turning the wedding and the married state into an idol. God planned for marriage to be a blessed state of mutual service to Him. The wedding is a beautifully decorated doorway into a house. The substance is found beyond the doorway in the house, which is the marriage relationship of husband and wife. Keeping this simple but important distinction is a protection from becoming too distracted and mesmerized by the doorway. The doorway should be beautiful, but, unfortunately, sometimes the relationship suffers during wrangles over cummerbund colors and guest lists. Our Lord graced a wedding at Cana with His presence; we want Him to be present at ours!

Another important consideration in wedding planning is the role of the bride and groom and parents: the bride and groom are the guests of honor at a big bash thrown by the bride's parents. Whoever is paying for this event is the one who decides what is going to happen. In other words, the bride and groom should defer to the bride's parents when it comes to wedding decisions. (Of course, if the bridal couple is paying for the wedding, this is not the case.) In the best situation, the parents will also be eager to defer to the couple. But the mindset of both bride and groom should be, "Mom and Dad, what kind of wedding do you want to give us?" This attitude prevents resentments, hurt feelings, and a host of other problems. Little temper tantrums can escalate into long-term difficulties. Most couples today assume that they can make all the decisions, and paying for it all is Dad's problem. This is not honoring father and mother. A wedding is a wonderful opportunity for children to honor and obey their parents as they leave to establish households of their own. A wedding should be God-honoring and parent-honoring, not a tense time of friction, worry, and unhappiness!

Finally, the world seeks to tempt us into wanting the perfect wedding unlike any other wedding in history. This temptation leads to a desire to out-do all our friends. "Our wedding" (or our daughter's wedding) "will have the . . ." best bridesmaids' dresses, the most unusual ceremony, the biggest party, the prettiest music, *etc.* This is nothing less than pride and covetousness. This is viewing the wedding as a spectacle, not as a celebration around a covenant. The focus should not be on impressing our friends, but on honoring Christ and celebrating a joyous occasion with our friends and family. We should want our friends to have a wonderful time, not be impressed with our expensive taste.

As Christians prepare and plan for weddings, we must think and behave like Christians. We must focus on God, the Creator of marriage, and honor Him in all our planning and celebrating, remembering how He has honored us with marriage as a picture of Christ and the Church.